BEYOND BRAND

Copyright © 2019 Joy Donnell
Published by SuperJoy Media

All rights reserved. No part of this publication may be reproduced, stored in a retrieval system, or transmitted, in any form or by any means, electronic, mechanical, photocopying, recording, or otherwise, without the prior written permission of the publisher, except in the case of brief quotations embodied in critical reviews and certain other noncommercial uses permitted by copyright law. Printed in the United States of America. For information and inquiries, call (424) 234-3648.

Set in 12/24 point Cormorant Garamond and 24/72 point Oswald

ISBN 978-1-7341243-0-9 (pbk)
ISBN 978-1-7341243-2-3 (aubk)

Library of Congress Control Number: 2019916131

Donnell, Joy
    Beyond Brand : master your power, joy, and media to live your legacy / Joy Donnell
Includes bibliographical references and index.

First printing edition 2019

JOY DONNELL
BEYOND BRAND

Master Your
POWER, JOY,
and MEDIA
To Live Your
LEGACY

SUPERJOY

For my niece Sydney and all those who seek, find, and endeavor to answer the restless calling that comes from within.

FRAMEWORK

PREFACE	x
INTRODUCTION	xi

Part 1: BEHOLD

01 | 7 Directions	3
02 | Even Media Has a Design	10
03 | Look Beyond Brand, You'll Find Legacy	19
04 | Brand or Cultural Legacy?	26
05 | Cultural Legacy As Sublime Wonder	32
06 | An Authentic Being	35
07 | Content Without Distribution Is Silence	38
08 | The Stories We Know Are Well-Funded	43
09 | Believe In Your Evolution	44
10 | Separate Your Voice From Your Thoughts	46
11 | Ego As Tool	49
12 | Strategy and Surrender	51
13 | Perspective x Perception	58
14 | Cultural Legacy As Trajectory	64
15 | Our Needs. Our Cultures.	66
16 | Owning It: Conviction	68
17 | Disrupting or Disrupted?	70
18 | Capital as Self-Efficacy	74
19 | Find the Source of Your Energy	77
20 | What the Ancestors Knew	80

21 | Not All Empathy Is Equal — 86
22 | All These Tropes — 91
23 | Pioneering is the Best Life Ever? — 95
24 | Oxytocin as Synchrony — 97
25 | Popularity Is Salience — 103
26 | Always Maintain Direct Contact — 107
27 | Visage. Voice. — 110
28 | Scale As Capital Gains — 113
29 | Make A Decision, Darling — 118
30 | The Question and Answer — 121

Part 2: BECOME

31 | The Primary Objective — 127
32 | Authority — 132
33 | A Fanbase. A Support Base. — 134
34 | Originality Is Overrated — 137
35 | Being Thought of Is Sublime — 142
36 | Networks Are Social Capital — 147
37 | Our Mentors Are Our Oracles — 149
38 | Our Detractors Provide Wisdom — 151
39 | Why Some May Oppose You — 153
40 | Allure Creates Its Own Myth — 157
41 | Say That — 160
42 | The Checklist — 166
43 | Alliance Is the New Hustle — 170
44 | Mentors Can Be Sponsors, Too — 178
45 | Spread Out — 182
46 | You Better Tell 'Em — 188
47 | Shut Up, Darling — 191
48 | Don't Feed the Frenzy — 195
49 | How To Release but Lay Low — 196
50 | Cycles — 197

51 | Repackage. Repurpose. Redistribute.	199
52 | Loot Your Content Bank	207
53 | Coups, Religions, and Drug Dealers	209
54 | Publicity Lessons from Despicable People	212
55 | Publicity Lessons from Admirable People	217
56 | The Shame Blame Game	222
57 | But Who's Winning the Narrative?	225
58 | Narrative Defense and Offense	227

Part 3: BEYOND

59 | Now	235
60 | A Luxury Mindset	238
61 | How the Process Feels	241
62 | Own Your Power	243
63 | Are You Having Fun, Darling?	249
64 | You're Creative Whether You Like It or Not	252
65 | Stay In Your Energy	254
66 | Finding Power In Uncertainty	257
67 | Cultivating Synchronicity	262
68 | Generational Gifts Further Legacy	265
69 | Self-Care Is a Leadership Skill	268
70 | In Case You Get Bored	271
71 | So, You've Become Attached?	273
72 | Amp Up the Allure	277
73 | Living Well	279
74 | Extra Is Beautiful	284
75 | Fortify Your Windows	288
76 | Keep Rising	291

Bibliography   295

Acknowledgments 300

About Beyond Brand 317
About Joy Donnell 318

> *You never change things by fighting against the existing reality. To change something, build a new model that makes the old model obsolete.*
> — BUCKMINSTER FULLER

> *If you want to learn about a culture, listen to the stories.*
> *If you want to change a culture, change the stories.*
> — MICHAEL MARGOLIS

> *In the end, we all become stories.*
> — MARGARET ATWOOD

Preface

This book doesn't have to be a linear journey unless you desire it to be so. It explores a fluid process of critical thinking rather than a step-by-step guide. These pages are observations and best practices intermingled with stories and meditative reflections. Within is an invitation to build from a mindset of growth rather than assembly. It will ask you to expand your approach to your vision and to how you operate within the media culture surrounding your life's work. This book asks you to have a sense of play as you go about fulfilling your purpose. It probes and poses questions, proposes ideas, and telescopes what is often taken for granted if not altogether ignored. Each chapter is a complete thought that relates to other complete thoughts. You can skip around, circle back, start in the middle, or jump to the end and work forward, and the ideas will interconnect. Scribble on the pages, journal in the back and make this book your own. This journey is yours.

Keep rising,
Joy Donnell

Introduction

Are we *really* supposed to be *personal brands?*

Some of our favorite companies are masters at branding. We love them for it. We worship them over it. We aspire to their cult-like status.

These companies carefully craft product identities and messages that connect human-made, inanimate objects to our deepest desires. These brands' logos and slogans accurately signal our emotions. By design, brands help products mimic our humanity. Branding exists to make things be more than just *things*. These things take on the qualities of people and, in some scenarios, reflect our ideals. Nowadays brands have "peopleness" and, in many cases, are considered to be far more vital to our daily lives than most actual people.

Multinational companies are brilliant at brand building. They have annual profits larger than most countries' treasuries. They're pillars of success. Few individual people can compete with the expansive, detailed branding of the corporate machine. Despite that disadvantage, people still strive and take cues from big business about how to achieve fiscal solvency. So, if corporate brands are a key mechanism of immense monetary success, it's a logical conclusion that a formidable personal brand can also do some damage in the world. Around the turn of our current millennia, individuals started to catch on to this idea. If a person wants to compete in the jungle of life, that person best build a personal brand.

But people aren't cans of soda. People are actually people and shouldn't have to mimic their own humanity. Yet, popular thought encourages the opposite mindset. Our societies proport, if not downright demand, that every entrepreneur, digital influencer, disruptor, change agent, rising celebrity or full-fledged star have a personal brand. This is now our normal.

The concept is messing with a lot of people's heads. It's creating a disconnect within our collective consciousness. It has folks stressed out and off-center. We're chasing validation over value, likes over like-mindedness, and solipsistic content over actual contribution.

I've greatly added to this confusion. I used to be a publicist with a firm in Beverly Hills, California. We handled luxury and entertainment, which included representing actual celebrities and emerging stars. Like everyone else, I pressured clients to mind their personal brands. I was helping them infuse their products — such as their movies, apparel lines, books and so on — with their unique image.

I always made an effort to maintain my client's humanity, regardless of whether we were crafting publicity photos, public appearances, packaging, a nonprofit initiative or a product launch. I knew to protect everyone's humanity. It's what I became known for; there's a distinction between brand building that only prioritizes profit, and building that elevates the being into a profitable entity. That distinction rarely gets a case study.

There's minimal existing language within our culture to lionize the concept.

All we talk about today is branding. Everyone is morphing into a personal brand so they can have a shot at money, status, and a stable future. It's priority #1 and the key strategy.

Personal branding is the new fame.

Recently, I overheard a 4 year old tell the woman who gave her life, "Mommy, I don't think that's on brand." The child is one year away from her personality fully forming but she already knows her brand. In our current climate, I'm not sure that feels odd. In fact, I doubt we've bothered to ask how we feel about any of this.

We're too busy fighting for our lives and livelihoods. It's survival of the fittest and anyone without a personal brand is someone to be pitied and dismissed. They're like that friendless kid eating cat poop out of the sandbox on the big playground of life. They're certainly never going to be King of the Hill. They definitely aren't the stuff of champions. Champions have brands that win.

Our obsession with branding is so ubiquitous that I had to put the word in this book's title just so people could begin to understand what I mean. We're fervently turning ourselves into things... into just brands. Nothing more. Nothing less. Yet, why would you want to take your complex, iridescent self and whittle <u>you</u> down to something as finite as a brand?

The corporation is supposed to mimic us, not the other way around. It's supposed to strive toward our innate humanity, not have us aspire toward its impersonation. We've embraced a Russian nesting doll of buffoonery.

I think we deserve to be more than brands. Since we're human, it's reasonable to think our methods and approaches should orbit around our whole human needs. Afterall, every endeavor we set out towards is a holistic journey and a chance at deeper self efficacy.

This is an invitation to an idea beyond brand. It's an opportunity to see the system for what it is and play with it rather than be played by it. This is growth strategy grounded in legacy.

If you've ever harbored a wild notion that you can affect change, or that your life energy has purpose, or that your work contributes betterment for us all, my proposal might be for you. If you're searching for insights on how to not only use media for your music or apparel or data or business startups, but also for expanding actual culture, consider this. Let's regain the power of our words, public images and actual humanity.

Trust but make this earn its keep. Challenge these thoughts. Buck against them. This isn't meant to be dogma. Demand they stay relevant to your human experience and if at any point any part of this book no longer serves you, rip the pages out and burn them. The idea is to increase our definitions, not brainwash us into static rigidity. Develop a flexible, mutable mindset.

Your approach is going to have to be uniquely yours. No one, including me, can tell you exactly what to do. You'll have to plan, launch, and adjust in real-time like everyone else. Your advantage, however, can be your information, knowledge and illumination.

Some universal truths about storytelling, social structures and collaboration have existed among us for over 100,000 years. We cannot separate the mind from the body, the person from the environment, or the culture from the context. They all inform each other. Honoring these truths can help us connect in ways that are bigger than branding. These are the truths that our ancestors perfected as they shared stories around the fire. These are truths that existed long before we had written records of our history. These facts tap into parts of our brains that haven't changed in 50,000 years. Combining what's ancient and vital with what's new and necessary in modern life can help your vision become a source of wonderment.

This book isn't about brand building. It's about legacy building. It focuses on a living cultural legacy, that is a cultural legacy you actually live right now with strategy, savvy and scale. It explores utilizing your voice, innovations, services, products and more to impart your gift to the world through an intricate system of media. We must understand what the system is, how it operates, what informs and influences it, and how it services our work.

The very second you become more than a brand, you make what you're doing bigger than a product. You make what you're doing a reflection of what exists in you. It helps you see further than what is anointed by technology or stymied by algorithms.

You're human. You deserve to become more than a brand. If you agree, keep reading.

Don't just think different. Think LEGACY.

PART ONE:

BEHOLD

01

7 Directions

Now. Listen. Media has become a basic human need. We easily die without our fundamentals: food, water, shelter, and clothing. Most people can only last 72 hours without water. You can definitely go longer than three days without media. However... if you desperately need water, don't know it's only 2 miles away and can't access the media that would provide that knowledge, you're as good as dead.

We don't think about our need for socialization and information sharing as a right, but solitary confinement wouldn't work as a torture device if there wasn't a build-in necessity. We take information for granted, which is why media doesn't feel like a need. We're biologically perfected to seek and share info but we don't pay much mind to media culture as the delivery system.

Yet, media's all around us. It's in our heads and the chatter of our minds. It's what we tell our friends over dinner or a phone call. Our phones and mobile devices overflow with it. Forms of media cover our buildings and sidewalks and magazine back covers. It's everything from gossip to graffiti, breaking news to blogs, and social media posts to movie posters.

Our world is too vast and fast to navigate without the system that media provides. Access and obstruction to information can literally mean life or death, equity or oppression, and opportunity for — or loss of — general wellbeing. Think of how many times a chance has passed you by simply because you didn't have the right information. That in and of itself is the power and necessity of media in the modern world. Human life is interdependent on media and we're simultaneously its audience, creators, and distribution portals.

We know the system has become bigger than us. This knowledge makes many feel virtually crushed by the Goliath of it all. Yet, the system is an extension of us. It's fueled by our stories and energies. Appreciating where we are helps us determine where we're going.

My grandmother taught me that life consists of seven directions: North, East, South, West, Up, Down and Here. This ancient viewpoint existed long before colonization and learning gave me more dimensions than the standard Western perspective of place and space. In her kitchen, she placed me on a wooden stool painted the color of bright sunshine and in that captivating spot I would hear all types of tales.

There were stories about how the world began. I learned about our family and the concept of inner power merging with innate gifts. Her words explored this repetitive idea of being present in nature, in my true self, and in my principles.

She could tell it like it is while also offering deep optimism.

See, my grandmother had raised a large black American family in the south during legalized segregation known as Jim Crow laws. Enduring such traumatic inequity gave her every right to always start in the past. Yet, her stories consistently began with, "Now. Listen." as a grounding for our need to be here. I like to believe that my grandmother held a hypothesis that nurturing my presence is how I would learn to value and uphold my limitless potential.

Much later, I would realize I was having my life enriched by oral tradition and the deep ancestry of storytelling. If it wasn't for storytelling and this ability we humans collectively have around narrative, media wouldn't even exist.

Long after her death, I've had to learn and relearn her lessons about the power of here. I've even used it to unlearn the false narratives of despair and prejudice. I often call upon her wisdom and her legacy to guide me during experiences of trauma, challenge, and intoxicating celebration. Her words are still able to reach across time and space to hold me when I feel utterly alone.

Here is also a direction. It's impossible to have any trajectory or speed of motion without starting here. Here is our beginning, and every great story requires an origin. The middle and the end won't happen without it.

Understanding *here* is how we gain **perspective, conviction, momentum, allure** and **clarity**. To create big things, we must start with small focus. We stand up alone but find many joining our side. We move ideas from vast intangible things inside our heads to material realities within our environment. Our environments factor into every aspect of what "being here" actually means.

We must strive to grasp our inner worlds as we shape our outer worlds. Everything we do is communication from the inside out and outside in. The ways we express, explore, engineer and design are informed by and emitting messages. The emotional catalysts of our words are the source code, regardless of how the languaging manifests. Every aspect of everything signals something. We're surrounded by and overloaded with such ceaseless sending and receiving that we're left with little time for deep self awareness.

We live lives that are constantly distracted from the power of here. This is disheartening when we realize that self awareness is what awakens a deep calling within us to contribute something to the world that's bigger than our individual life. It's our self compassion that expands our compassion for others and drives us to endeavor in causes, campaigns, cultural shifts, and cultural experiences that will elevate us as a whole.

Modern life is crowded and dense. Our population has exploded and technology has made global news as accessible as local. We're called upon to live internationally and think in abstract communities and groups. We're tasked with simultaneously building communities in three dimensional life and the digital space while also (somehow) remaining staunch individuals. We're expected to be originally interesting 24/7 and, above all else, be a brand. Someone somewhere declared an edict that everyone must build a strong personal brand.

Branding is popular and that popularity has gained so much momentum that we don't even question the utility. We keep equate influence with insight and trend with significance. So, we no longer ponder if using 25 percent of our waking life force to build a personal brand is the true work of a human life. Brand, which is all about profitable public image, feels like accessible fame.

In our zeitgeist, a soupçon of fame is the only way any of us can begin to compete for attention and opportunity among billions of other people. Those who can gather the largest followings, create the most scintillating or engaging content, and drive the most traffic get anointed with the most media attention and subsequent fame. Branding has become part of the fame game, but they aren't inherently conscious. They borrow conscious attributes. Brands are missing the magic of the human variable.

Personal branding is a smart part of individual business strategy and development, but it can't be the entire plan. Branding has legitimate ethics around truthfulness and deliverables. However, there's still something wanting in terms of a deep socio cultural imperative.

Mass media is our most powerful storytelling delivery system. Brands are mixed up in the narrative but we aren't talking about how they influence us. Throughout history, a lot of "branding" has gone into creating exclusionary spaces and places.

Racism, sexism, religious persecution, homophobia, xenophobia and numerous other "-isms" restricted who would get documented and who wouldn't. The constructs constricted who had history and who didn't, who got to preserve legacy and whose lineage got systematically written out of books, excluded from the screen, edited from branded assets, and misreported in news.

In the worst cases, censorship and restrictive covenants actually got placed in laws, policies and codes of conduct to legally and morally exclude certain bodies from spaces, places, betterment opportunities, and media. They stifled our collective creativity. Whole legacies have been lost because the gifted were weighed down by other people's crap.

When certain identities get excluded from the media simply because of their bodies and the lack of belief about their credible humanity, they start to learn that society sees them as wrong. They are unfit misfits. Their power of here tries to get warped and discredited as if their unique experiences don't hold weight.

Perhaps all this documenting we're doing through new technologies isn't just vainglory. We may be in a struggle to reclaim and reassert the factual diversity that has been so long denied within our collective story. To do this, we need to go beyond branding alone. We need to harness some legacy mojo.

What if we have an ethical obligation to reclaim cultural legacies that have been unethically marginalized? What if we have a human imperative to utilize the most powerful storytelling delivery system we possess to expand our cultural narratives and societal ideas about our collective potential? Is it possible that our future survival will depend on more data, information, knowledge and wisdom that can be gathered from our complex and naturally diverse experiences? What if we absolutely must expand our cultural legacies so that more individuals can imagine more possibilities for themselves and our humanity as a whole?

Our complex world demands collaboration, and just like storytelling, thinking is a collaborative process. Our range of thinking is limited by what we know, what we don't know, what we don't notice and what we fail to acknowledge. The media system itself doesn't value one over another. So, those who approach media with cultural legacy in mind have an extraordinary opportunity. Understanding the system is one step, but understanding your passion and beliefs is how you find the messaging to move your vision through the system.

You'll need to behold the gift and capacity of perspective. It will be key to expanding ideas of assets, distribution, alliances, and the strategy for vocabulary building, opposition handling, and narrative momentum. As your vision becomes more, doubt will serve as a helpful tool. Alliances and community can provide moments of lift. Salience becomes more potent. Strategy and automation combine to increase possibilities. The feeling of being alone and a little uncertain is often a sign you're heading in the right direction, for you've dared to ask new questions and do different things.

As momentum increases and possibilities advance beyond what was previously imagined, more strategy is required around capital resources, power and diversification of this legacy. Energy keeps things moving and shifting. Your goal is to learn how to shift with it, maintain your self-kindness, and let everything evolve.

It's essential to remember that a brand will never have the dynamic articulation of your actual personhood. As a golem, brands are never as flexible as us. They can never use the structure of media in the unique ways an individual person can and therein lies the real opportunity. So let's begin.

02

Even Media Has Design

Media. It's almost easier to say what it isn't. At its core, media is communication and expression. I can't imagine a world without all of us constantly abstracting what we experience in life into some form of content. The system of media has evolved to utilize everything imaginable as a messenger.

If we want to interpret the design of the media system, then we have to ask how it communicates. We have to perceive its cultural norms and behaviors alongside the context within which these elements operate. Design is the communication of the object's utility — so where and how it's useful, profitable and beneficial all matter, concurrently.

Since the system is validated or venerated by culture, the ways that people seek out data determines what media is and where it goes. It defines popularity by crowd size and knows that money exists wherever people gather for information. That gathering can be digital or physical. So, this system branches out where funds are invested. Advertising and marketing opportunities aid distribution which makes a branch of the system viable so that it can become, grow and sustain.

Many people eagerly begin using media for promotion and popularity without fully examining how the environment's fabric is woven overall. They'll gain large visibility on one channel and little visibility on another because they don't understand how the system works collectively. They only figure out one platform at a time. Looking at the elements and avatars of content helps us determine an outline for deeper insight.

For the purposes of our conversation, I'll illustrate what elements I see in the media system. Just like design, media is grounded in sensory experiences. That includes content that is: Visual, Tastable, Tangible, Smellable and Audible. Our senses are at the foundation of media's system, too. The roots, a.k.a. oral tradition, began as something that was purely experiential. You had to be there in person to hear the tale. Eventually, we got the written word and visual arts that kept the stories experiential but also made them portable and *present* without an active storyteller.

Aside from actual experiential content that can be consumed in person, digital offers more possibilities than other forms of media for creating full sensory moments. We don't yet have ways to transport smell, touch or taste digitally, but all of that is being worked on as a goal. Take the presence of ASMR video and audio. Whispering voices on video/audio can create an Autonomous Sensory Meridian Response, or tingling sensation along the scalp and back of the neck resulting in an overall sense of well-being, without actually being touched. It's the digital

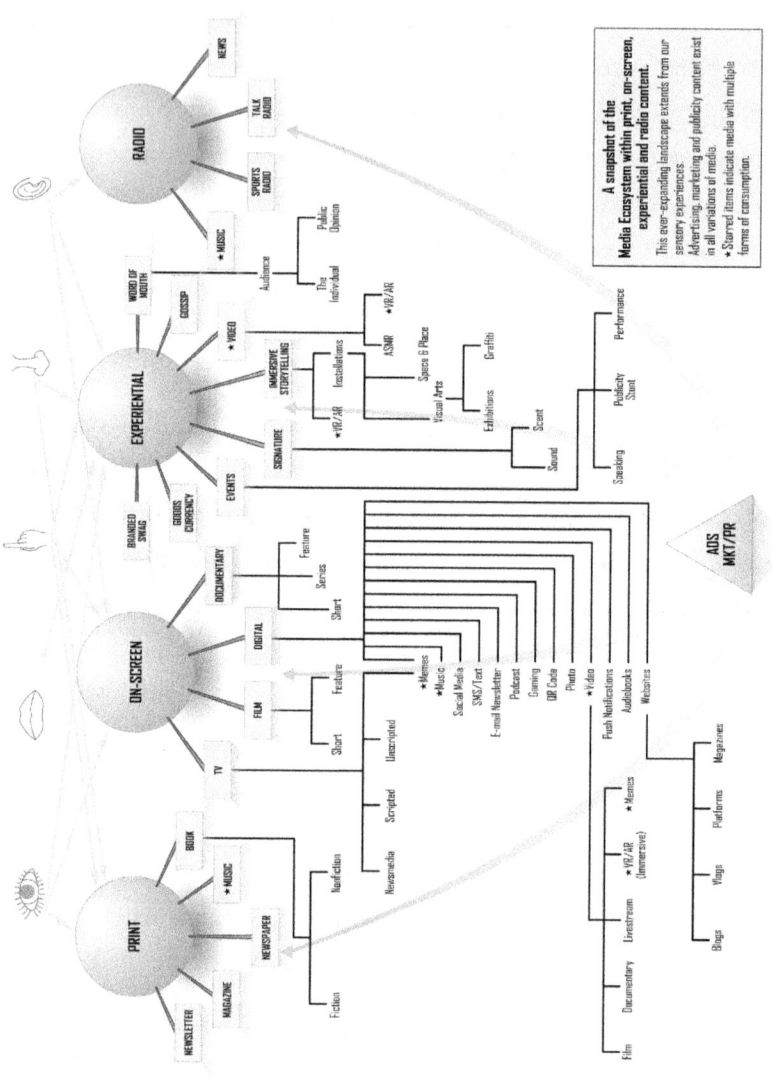

equivalent of a scalp massage.

Until digital transmission is perfected for all sensate experiences, combinations are needed to connect with people on multiple sensory levels. Through Print, On-Screen, Experiential and Radio content, media connects with our senses. From these main categories, every type of content we can ever make will fall.

Our newspapers can be print, digital and radio content all at once. Our TV shows can also offer swag apparel, SMS alerts, and pop-up experiences that tour the country. Our radio show can become an art installation, email newsletter, and documentary while the show's logo can be transformed into graffiti mural backdrops for people to take cool photos in front of at a launch party. Anything and everything from a business venture to a cultural awareness campaign can use any of these aforementioned elements in unique ways to craft distinctive, monetizable content.

Content drastically varies in its forms, but the one constant is that every variation of content can easily be utilized as advertising/marketing/publicity. This trifecta is interlaced with the entirety of modern media and is present within every aspect of it. Anyone can focus solely on how to make something popular so that it will gain momentum — a "build it and they will come" approach — but understanding that money is always required creates clearer strategy. Monetize it and the system will reward it. Monetize it and momentum will continue to fuel it.

The stories we know are the stories that got funded. Distribution needs money and is money. It requires momentum and is momentum. It works in concert with ads, marketing and publicity to gain the holy grail: word of mouth and presence in the mind.

Distribution exists to help a person, place or thing gain space in your thoughts and the possibility of your consumerism when the time comes. The system's interdependence with funds and funding means few things still experience organic media growth, if there was ever such a thing in the first place. Even though the system's barriers to entry have lessened, the forethought required to properly appreciate and navigate the entity's range of possibilities has increased tremendously.

Back when I was a teenager with a newly minted license to drive, I got sideswiped by an unexpected rule. Before my dad would let me drive my car, I had to know how to change a tire, check the oil and fluids, and understand the concept of changing the oil. In his opinion, and eventually within my own, it was a better idea to know some basic things about car maintenance before getting on the road with such a powerful machine. The more I knew about a vehicle, the harder it was to get swindled by a shady mechanic, discouraged by a minor issue, or even stranded helpless on the side of the road to be dependent upon the kindness of strangers.

We live in an extraordinary time where we can use all types of tech and devices at our will. We don't have to know how to design microchips to use a mobile phone or even ascertain how the phone actually works. The tool does our bidding and when it stops functioning, we swap it out for a new one.

We dive into media and distribution the same way, but our personal feelings around gains and losses are very different. When our messaging isn't well received or acknowledged to exist, it feels like an attack on our souls. It creates existential crisis because our hopes around career growth, personal growth and tangible success are wrapped up in the ability to connect in prosperous ways with others. It rarely occurs to us that some of the disappoint may stem from getting on the road without understanding basic things about the car.

There seems to be an invisible committee determining mainstream media at any given moment. Brave individuals with ideas worth sharing need to enter the media space at ideal entry points in order to avoid misery. These starting points have momentum and opportunity. The momentum results from countless others having already driven tons of money into the flow of a particular story and thought process. This financial fuel existed way before the new individual came along with a fresh story.

The opportunities are in riding the current wave and/or finding the gaps in the media that will feed a different, vital and hungry audience that has been underserved by the current content available. This is a group waiting to be recognized as mainstream. Like all living beings, they want opportunity for growth and to see themselves reflected back. It's an unusual cruelty to have an entire ocean of experience and yet be treated like you are simply a drop of water. When a fresh story that better serves them gets marketed properly to this group, they show up with their money, time and energy. Once the media system realizes this new perspective is being funded, things open up and change.

Some people are only able to find an extra $25 a month to publicize their efforts while a small business might use up $10,000 a year in advertising and some conglomerates, like LVMH, easily enjoy an annual marketing budget of over $400 million. Yet, having money is one thing. Knowing how to spend it with savvy is another.

The most strained resources can go far with smart strategies around sensory experience-driven content, the proper entry point for the message, the right targeting for audience growth, efforts that involve multiple levels of outreach, and content that is easy to distribute between the people that will make up the message's community. When specificity is lifted by a well-organized strategy, growth becomes inevitable. That growth will prove to the system that the message is more universal than previously acknowledged and the momentum will attract more momentum.

Media flows, connects, and gets funded in patterned clusters. The *groupings* and the *gaps* both hold opportunities to build audience. People are either already being served or are underserved by the messages that surround them. Let the system's momentum help you connect to <u>your</u> audience. Turn that audience into a community.

Within your *specificity* is the *universality*. Messages are magnetic. What you put out will come back to you. The way you use words and define ideas will determine what avenues of media you can utilize. So be *mindful* of your vocabulary and the narrative you build. Powerful storytelling doesn't just relate. It resonates.

03

Look Beyond Brand, You'll Find Legacy

Beholding the vast possibilities of the media system shows that brand mentality exalted above all else is especially limiting concept for a living breathing person. Humans are capable of more extraordinary things than being branded. Developing a successful brand is a pinnacle of achievement for a corporation because that entity is only defined as a "person" under the eyes of the law and the belief of the society. Corporatized things must mimic humans and beg us for our energy. They practically hypnotize us into believing they are like us.

Somehow, we've started trying to mimic the thing that's trying to mimic us. Yet, it feels like heresy to think that your existence doesn't have to be confined and defined by a personal brand. Humans, while not very old in relation to the cosmos, are ancient compared to branded images.

Humans are capable of being change agents, thought leaders,

activists and innovators. We can express the truth of existence through any artform and motivate a crowd of one million to action simply through our visionary words. We are the forces that shift behaviors, environments and norms. To limit our abilities to something finite like a brand is a disservice to human advancement and spiritual growth. Branding should be a vehicle, not the sole destination.

If you look beyond brand, you'll find legacy. When most of us think "legacy" we think financial inheritance, family names on buildings and street signs, perhaps even an endowment or trust. That's the method we conjure in our minds but the motivation behind the thought is to leave something of benefit that lives on. We see legacy as a way to leave something behind that will continue to better those we love.

When I state *legacy*, I mean a *calling* to do something that extends beyond your solipsistic life. I mean art you feel compelled to create, politics you want to change, and human rights you strive to win or protect. I mean a fiery mandate you believe you should answer to serve as a bridge to what is possible for humanity and culture. This is wishing to contribute beyond your family and friends.

Our cultural legacies impact our daily lives. These legacies still travel through the veins of media as they tell, shape and reconfigure modern stories. Cultural legacy coupled with financial legacy is one of the most powerful forces known.

Take Rumi, for example. This Persian poet and Sufi master died in 1273. Yet in 2014, some 741 years after his death, Rumi was the best-selling poet in the United States. That's not taking into account his legion of fans worldwide.

Rumi is making more money dead than most people make

while breathing and, to top things off, he has books, coffee mugs, clothing and more to remind you of his enduring messages. How is someone so long in the ground so vital to the living? In Rumi's case, it helps that he was a wealthy nobleman with the time to be prolific. From 37 to 67 years old he wrote 3,000 love songs and 2,000 rubayat focused on love, self knowledge, self acceptance and the path toward a full human experience.

Herein lies the opium of it all. Our cultural legacies endure longer when they tap what we seek, how we search, what we find and how we grow. As we embark on interstellar existence, rapidly advance our technology, become less tethered to Earth's gravity and the fleshly limitations of our bodies, knowing how to live life becomes more challenging.

We can ask Google or Siri just as easily as we ask a priest or a mystic, yet our advancements have a way of making us feel less free, less connected and less actualized. Life is becoming increasingly complex, so we yearn for what is simple within ourselves. We continuously seek our teachers and guides through this esoteric structure that we didn't create. We voraciously need any knowledge we can gain about navigating oppression, inequity, angst, happiness...

I began producing, speaking and writing because I want to focus on cultural legacy. I like to create media that increases humanity, speaks to social justice, deepens cultural understanding and expands self awareness. Throughout the years, I've worked with many clients who wish to expand cultural legacy through their work/art, activism, philosophy, innovations, books and more. I've used media and the system as an assistant to that goal.

This all boils down to storytelling. As Judithe Registre so

eloquently summarizes in her **Inclusivus** podcast slogan: "Our stories shape our beliefs and our beliefs become our reality." We have almost endless generations of storylines and tropes that have defined the parameters for our societies, rituals and self identities. It's become difficult to know what's now nature and what's still nurture. Story breeds and reinforces culture. So the narrative is the foundation of cultural legacy.

There's no guarantee that what you offer will hold enduring relevance or that your intention will be your actual impact. It doesn't matter, either. The desire to contribute a verse to this illustrious song of humanity, a verse that serves humanity, is a worthwhile endeavor. The path requires strategy and surrender, promotion and protection, resiliency, community, focus and funding.

The pain, joy, pleasure, suffering, loss and discovery will all shape you. The process will forge you into something you can't yet imagine. You're supposed to become unrecognizable because this is a transformation that inspires transformation. This is change that sparks deeper change. The change is you, right here, where you are. It will become the messages and content you generate. It will shift the way you relate to media's design in general. It will dramatically alter the way you talk to people, whether they be your audience or your collaborators.

This endeavor demands devotion to inner work. The journey can be bliss just as easily as it can be despair. You can get caught up in being celebrated just as easily as you get distracted by being criticized. How you see things will be shaped by your mindset, your relationship to stressors, and your remembrance of your core passion and motivation. Keeping yourself vibrant through maintaining relationships with people, versus devoting all your time to tasks, is essential. Finding balance is required.

Your vocabulary is going to be bucked against. Expand it. Vocabulary is another form of seeing. You question perceptions and stay agile with your perspective. Such agility can be the thing that helps you stay whole despite the things trying to make you break.

WHATEVER *you* **BELIEVE** is what *you will* BUILD.

Because you're *here to* **CREATE** and *will* create everyday your journey is *yours to* **DECIDE.**

04

Brand or Cultural Legacy?

S ome truisms are tricky. They walk and talk like the truth but they're actually rhetoric in disguise. They get passed down and passed around without ever being investigated and eventually, the systems of thought that support them become systems of actions to make them truer through practice and application. There's a current argument that everyone needs to build a personal brand. Without one, your future is murky.

This gets further muddled by the rise and widening of celebrity. Celebrity is a phenomenon that even celebrities can't reliably explain. It usually stems from being known for excelling at a thing such as acting, singing, modeling, etc. It's a surreal existence that is almost equal to deifying or canonizing the living. Something about all that recognition makes us imagine it's a path to being cared for and protected.

In general, humans just want to be seen and valued. We want our basic needs to be met. We want to feel empowered and self actualized through our own self determination. We desire enough security to find calm within our conscious experience and enough chaos to experience playful surprise so things don't get dull. We wish to live lives of purpose and meaning. We want to leave the world better than how we found it. We just want to be OK. There's nothing simple about these needs and desires. Their existence manifests a ton of ambivalence within us individually and together.

Many of us have started regarding fame and branding, and the envisioned success that these two things promise, as our ultimate end goals. Pop Culturally, they've become the apotheosis of a secure and meaningful life because fame and branding feels more accessible than ever before.

So what, who cares and why does any of this matter? You can build a brand or endeavor towards leaving a legacy. You can do nothing at all. The sun will still rise and set. It doesn't turn water into wine. Why spend so much effort and human capital on doing anything?

There's something within us that's always trying to balance individualism with community belonging. It's not easy, especially if your community looks at your beingness as something that should be cured rather than celebrated. Both being an outsider and a joiner come with pressure.

Going it alone is a chance to carve out your own life. None of this changes a very real issue: no civilization has been able to last without putting thought into future generations and making deliberate choices that gift these forthcoming beings with a better chance at life. Some sacrifice has to be made, but we don't want to be martyred, and rightfully so.

Building a brand, for some people, is sheer martyrdom. I argue that launching a cultural legacy instead is a way to benefit the future while also doing your best to care for yourself. We've started to realize that all human endeavor requires a holistic methodology or the human at the center of the goal will literally crumble.

Brands are just images and abstractions making money. They require nothing that demands a human remain whole and intact. An image does not, by itself, make any legacy, let alone a cultural one.

A cultural legacy is more than imagery and brand attributes. It extends from human thought, emotion and connectivity. It holds assets and has collateral. The assets help monetize its stamina, but the assets, alone, do not define it. Its presence in the narrative landscape of culture and its desire to be an intergenerational gift is what defines it.

Brands are just a form of cash. They're assets with no obligation to endure or contribute anything other than money and the moment they stop making money, they cease being assets. So anyone who has a public image that isn't making money, has only that — a public image, not a brand.

A cultural legacy is an ecosystem. At its best, it combines ideology, insight, cultural distinction, community harmony, holistic resonance and capital to give your beneficiaries a better chance at winning in life. If anything, a brand is part of the cultural legacy, one asset in a bounty of many.

Brands typically have 2 options in the pathways of media. At any given moment, a brand is either regarded as:

Advertising or *Entertainment*.

By this choice, I mean that a brand is either paying for the spotlight or it's being so interesting and newsworthy that the spotlight is bestowed upon it. While all news can be considered media, not all media is news. Yet, not even the news can function without making money. So the demand for scintillating, amusing, shocking and overall entertaining segments and news items is skyrocketing. The news, and general media, treats every piece of boring content from a brand as advertising and the moment it gets seen as such, a brand's going to have to pay for visibility.

These pay-to-play opportunities can coincide with the methods of normal advertising through media buys, sponsored content, or product placement. They can also differ dramatically in presentation, such as a traditional banner ad, interactive augmented reality ad or a branded content editorial. Make the content deliciously entertaining and the media system will use it in a news cycle and promote it for free as newsworthy/trending. This entertaining aspect can be positive (generating praise for the brand) or negative (evoking deep, scathing criticism of the technique or topic). Either way, the goal is to be cool enough to generate views, and the engagement of a gawking audience. Engagement is the endgame, and the engagement the brand should seek is a buying or consumption event. This is why they have to pay-to-play.

A **BRAND** IS A
PUBLIC IMAGE
OR IDENTITY THAT IS REGARDED AS AN ASSET.

It has to make money to hold value.

A **CULTURAL LEGACY** IS AN

IDEOLOGICAL GIFT

THAT CONTRIBUTES INTERGENERATIONALLY.

At least 3 generations, to be exact.

05

Cultural Legacy as Sublime Wonder

Within media, cultural legacy dances with the heartspace in ways pure brands never can. Brands don't give us hope that we're full of purpose or make us feel flawed; that's what culture does. The best cultural legacies are a visceral experience. They erupt emotions within us to the extent that they feel like logic. They script our advertising and entertainment while also transcending it by flowing with culture itself, not just trends.

This variation helps cultural legacy tap into the sublime and wonder of being human by battling what's best of ourselves with what's worst. It searches ideas of heroes, villains and the underlying tropes present in almost every story of a society. It finds its way into other people's philosophies, art, and interviews. It touches on every aspect of media from blogs to banner ads. It changes how we document our existence.

Cultural legacy is regarded one way by the media. As:

Sublime Wonder.

Sublime storytelling is the way a narrative connects to the audience's ever-present need for wonder. Group dynamics reinforce this sensation of tapping into what is greater than us. Humans long to be part of something that feels bigger than themselves and because living is so uncertain, we obsessively seek an answer to life itself. Whether we admit it or not, we treat everything that feels like a life path as a magical way to become more. Go to a surgeon with a physical issue and the suggestion will most likely be surgery, for this person have derived surgery and medicine as an answer to life's mysteries.

That's why cultural legacies are recognized as guidance through the maze of life. They can be a part of both advertising and entertainment while also being beyond these tiny categories. They almost feel like what Marx might have called "the opium of the people."

Cultural legacy embodies our complex human saga in a way branded advertising alone simply can't. It's a way to separate information from illumination. Cultural legacy actually supplies the underlying story the brand attempts to tap so that its story mimics human attributes.

That's the denotative difference, but there's also a connotative one. I speak globally about publicity, branding, entrepreneurship and media. A few years ago, as social media presence became imperative for entrepreneurs and public figures, I started getting a question I'd never been asked before.

The question threw me. I didn't even understand it, at first:

"As I grow my brand, how do I maintain my authenticity?"

For me, asking how to maintain authenticity is as counterintuitive as asking, "How can I plan to be more spontaneous?" You simply are.

I'm never asked about authenticity when I discuss legacy building. That's not a coincidence. People don't embrace the idea of legacy without knowing what truly matters, first and foremost. In fact, cultural legacy begins with a deep sense of knowing and it thrives through an endless yearning to know even more. It has a calm and restlessness that is intoxicating to those who seek the same. Legacy also knows exactly where it draws the lines. While it may amend goals when they don't materialize as is, it doesn't negotiate the non-negotiables.

Authenticity is paramount to knowing and tapping your truth. You tap it so deeply that you shout it from the rooftops ad nauseum, ad infinitum. People don't seem to have the same obligation to the truth of themselves when it comes to building that personal brand.

It's as if there's an unspoken acceptance that the brand has to exist by any means necessary, hence it ceases to hold value, so any myth will do as long as it keeps funding the bank account. The problem is that it's hard to keep up a lie, and as soon as the facade is perceived to slip, journalists and onlookers amplify it into scandal and crisis.

We see lines whether we can verbalize them or not and regardless of whether our behavior reflects our actual desires.

06

An Authentic Being

It's not your job to be a brand. If you want to own brands as part of your revenue streams, I think that's brilliant. If you want to have a personal brand, I'm not discouraging that. My point is, there's nothing about the human experience that's going to convince me you exist on this planet to just be a brand or be restricted and imprisoned by your public image. I'm not convinced you're here to live a life where your progress and complexities are constantly usurped by your obligation to "be on brand." Additionally, if the investment into brand building isn't yielding the proper fiscal return, I start to question if all this energy channeled into feeding a brand that has yet to *become* is just a distraction from the real work.

Once you realize it's not your job to be a brand, your energy shifts. You embrace the cultural legacy you wish to build. You don't wonder how to be authentic. You are authentic. You don't kowtow to trends. You exist beyond them. You tell your unique story. You create your world.

It seems that inauthentic tendencies arise when an individual doesn't reconcile that their image is an idea. You have your self-image which you perceive through your behavior. There's also your ideal self, or who you strive to be. Then there's your social self, the way that others interpret you. You'd think that's enough, but there's also your ideal social self-concept: the perception of your image as you'd like others to have of you.

Sometimes, brands understand these various aspects better than actual people. See, brands mimic humanness due to one basic belief that a person will choose a brand whose image is close to his or her self-image. This is self-congruity as a form of brand personality, or the human traits and principles a brand takes on for symbolic or value effectiveness.

The head scratcher is how easily we dismiss our own value in pursuit of the ideal social self-concept. All those cool things about you that you deem too weird and throw down into the gutter, some brand will pick up, put on and make a billion dollars with it.

Your life's inner work is to get as fully acquainted with your truths (and lies) as possible. Most of us find this to be grueling. The exhaustion is the push and pull between what's being said inside our heads combined with what's happening in the world around our bodies.

So, we can ignore it, work around it, and avoid it, but none of this human stuff flows without self compassion. Lack of self compassion will make you do inauthentic things just as easily as it'll keep you from forgiving yourself when you do them. Lack of self compassion can make you afraid to take up space in the world. Or it can make you demand your presence be seen where/when it's not necessary and impeding progress. You'll do things that are downright shamelessly shameful, and that mess causes its own buffoonery.

Self compassion has its own style. Authenticity becomes a state of being when you own yourself, remember who you are in the face of difficulty and show up for yourself with kindness and patience. Yet, none of this has a focal point if you don't accept the fact that you will always change, that your present self can rarely fathom your future fully and properly, and you must allow yourself to change because life — which you are an expression of — is always supposed to grow.

07

Content Without Distribution Is Silence

We instinctively know that the delivery system for our narratives is interconnected with ads, marketing and publicity. That's why modern culture values fame, eyeballs and word of mouth so much. The current proverb states, "Content is King." Well, Distribution is Queen, darling. Content without distribution is silence. For this very reason, cultural legacy requires monetization beyond the fiscal solvency that a brand alone can provide. To achieve this, you need a strategy that can be scaled.

The web of media has always been too daunting without strategy. While some outliers managed to make their way through it by sheer luck, most of the names you know as legend had a plan. Most of the ideological shifts you know had investors of time, money and social capital. It wasn't all coincidence and serendipity.

Two twentieth century masters of media planning were Houdini and the Reverend Dr. Martin Luther King, Jr. Although they couldn't be more different (one was a magician and the other was a Nobel Peace Prize-winning activist) they both knew how to use the media system to document and broadcast their actions and beliefs around the world.

Both expertly alerted the media before any public happenings. Houdini knew how to use his own body and physical performance as marketing through publicity stunts such as getting free from a straight jacket while hanging upside down. Dr. King was able to harness his electrifying speeches, peaceful public protests, and innate writing ability to acquire global publicity for the Civil Rights Movement. Considered a masterpiece, his civil rights manifesto "Letter from a Birmingham Jail" was also widely published in newspapers throughout the United States. Neither of these icons had social media or digital media as a tool for their work. If social media had existed for these icons, don't you think they would have used it?

Our difference, today, is the playing field we now enjoy via accessible technology. In the past, mastering two to three aspects of media made you really good. Four or five techniques made you a bona fide unicorn. Now, you need to be fluent in at least a dozen aspects to have a snowball's chance at longevity. This isn't for the short sighted and there are no shortcuts.

Throughout this process, you will always be a storyteller. You have no choice. Aside from making things and providing care, sharing information and wisdom is essentially all we collectively do as a species.

Looking deeply into yourself and understanding the structure of media to provide energy to our efforts are a simultaneous process. Once you respect the ubiquity and undeniable value of storytelling, you'll recognize how to provide your messaging with a beginning, a middle, and an end.

That structure will need 3 elements:

1. **Intent:** that is is a clear, clean, concise construct that serves as your central mantra. It can shift over time, but it always holds center to vocabulary and content you create.

2. **Intensity:** this is the source of the energy and the magic. It mixes mystery with mission. It uses repetition to increase validity and veracity. It is the connective sublime. It is the buoyancy that inspires others to join your efforts, which results in moments of life and synchronicity.

3. **Integration:** your narrative has to find homes within the heart and mind. It has to align with the like-minded. It has to challenge the opposite. It has to threaten to replace what has become tired and obsolete.

It will be impossible to plan everything. Let that go. Yes, some things will have to be left to chance. Other moments will require surrender and acceptance of what can't be changed. Whatever can be finessed had best be so. This is especially true if what you endeavor towards is progress.

Progress is never permanent. It's always endangered by opposition that wants to replace it with something else. Capital and marketing are the perfect tools to protect it.

Everything you want to grow requires *money* and *mouths* in order to thrive.

The Stories We KNOW Are The Ones That Got FUNDED

financial resources + human capital energize narratives.

08

The Stories We Know Are Well-Funded

The stories we know are the stories that got funded. We do a disservice to our very energy and effort when we ignore the truth about progress. Progress is always at war. As long as someone remembers and longs for what once was, there will always be resistance to what can be.

Progress never feels like progress to everyone, so it is perpetually under threat. The larger our population grows, the more distinct opinions will exist about what progress is. Cultural shifts seen by a majority as gains can easily be under siege from an infuriated, frightened, well organized few.

While those who are happy with change sleep soundly through the night, the opposition restlessly implements a plan. Cultural narratives and ideological legacies are the weapons of choice to derail progress. So while we usually credit people with shaping culture, it's just as often the other way around.

09

Believe in Your Evolution

You can't only invest in the work. You must also invest in you. Investing yourself requires belief in your future self. Allow yourself to evolve and believe in your evolution.

If that last sentence seems obtuse, you're either:

a) lying (to yourself and others)

b) not owning your unique expression of life

Most people are never going to be 100% authentic 24 hours a day, 7 days a week. I'm not even sure that's the goal. Life's too complex with hierarchies, bureaucracies, and stupidity for complete and total authenticity to be an actual thing.

If you can discover some comfort in the realization that your sense of self fluctuates and is in many ways a fragile notion, that's the first step toward being as authentic as possible. Most of the time, all you have is what you remember about existing as you, and that's based on what you know about existing at the time. It takes a lot of inner work, study and seeking to live a full human experience, let alone accomplish huge dreams. But investing in yourself requires actual belief in the existence of your future self. Believe your evolution. Believe, even when it's disparaging and messy. If you do it well enough, at some point, you exceed your own doubts and expectations — you become unrecognizable.

10

Separate Your Thoughts From Your Voice

EXERCISE #1

HEAR YOURSELF.

An unflinching devotion to self-awareness is an act of rebellion in the 21st century. Yet, maintaining your authenticity is impossible if you don't know how to hear yourself and recognize who you are during situations and circumstances.

I've found that my inner voice and my thoughts aren't the same thing. My inner voice — true voice — sounds like me and absolutely always talks to me sweetly. My thoughts, however, are all the noise from within and without: lofty brilliance mingling with absolute trash. I work daily on separating my voice from my thoughts so that when my inner voice speaks, I hear it better each time. The more skillfully I listen, the more I'm reminded of myself, my aspirations, and my inner joy. This makes it easier to release what isn't mine and speak with centered clarity. It makes me a better creative and storyteller.

Here's a list of Daily Habits to Separate Thoughts from Your True Voice. You can start with the first three steps and bring them into your daily process until they become natural. Then add the next two steps and lastly, the final four exercises. Lather, rinse, repeat and build upon for a cumulative effect.

BEGIN WITH:

1. **Set Your Day's Intentions**. Before interacting with any devices or work obligations.

2. **Write Out** 5 things for which you're Passionate.

3. **Spend 5** minutes on Positive Self-Talk about your passions.

NOW ADD:

4. **Use Your Voice**. Talk about 1 thing each day that you feel deserves/needs your voice/energy.

5. **Empower Your Silence**. Identify 1 thing that doesn't deserve your energy and then don't give it any energy.

AND FINALLY:

6. **Find 1 Thought** that's holding you back.

7. **Identify** where that thought originated.*

8. **Forgive Yourself** for that thought.

9. End your day with **Gratitude**.

Some thought origins are discovered in layers and identifying where it was derived will be revealed in baby steps. In order to not get stuck on this step, focus on forgiving yourself for the thought, regardless of its origin. The main purpose of this exercise is to discover whether that thought came from within you or was given to you by someone else so that you know how to release it.

II

Ego As Tool

Your ego is either your tool or your master. It's often vilified as the culprit of inner wildness and outer destructive societal behavior. Perhaps it is. However, I don't think the ego is a lesser form of our individual selves; I find it to be a part of thought, and thought is a collaborative process. We are a species with vast neurodiversity. Some of us have vibrantly detailed mind's eyes. Others of us have aphantasia and can't visualize images in our own heads. All of our brains work differently, but, for the most part, we collectively have ego.

Certain parts of us gather data, like our senses. Other parts struggle to convert that data into information, information into knowledge, and knowledge into wisdom. We struggle towards all these pieces becoming a sum total illumination. Ego grapples with what we know, what we fear, and what we want while also striving to preserve and protect the self identity. It's very sensitive to inequity, whether you're suffering it or benefiting from it.

The ego is what helps you not only think that something must be said, but that you are, in fact, the person who should say it. This doesn't mean the ego should do press interviews or pick up a camera to shoot a video. When your ego takes over, you say things you'll later regret. Ego-driven interviews lead to apology tours. The ego shouldn't create your media strategy because it will keep the plan vain and overly sensitive, like an exposed nerve.

Yet, it can be harnessed as a barometer. Instead of giving it free reign when it's overactive, pause instead and question the inner conflict. This is an opportunity for self examination. You should question what is causing you so much stress and suffering.

The ego can also serve as a source of big, bold thinking. It can be a part of you that thinks, "enough waiting for someone else to do it." It helps you nurture the audacity to believe you can do more than others imagine for you. It can help you believe that you are your own revolution. The ego can be tapped to infuse your words with raw emotionality, soul-stirring imagery, and the type of energy that ignites others. You just have to know how to get quiet and listen without it taking control.

12

Strategy and Surrender

Our world is not only concerned with what you say, but also with how you say it. Doing media outreach without a plan opens doors to disappointment and wasted time. Media culture is overflowing with splintering, polarization, posturing and positioning that will easily back you into corners if you jump in without any strategy whatsoever.

Content is a hypnotic, persuasive force. Not devising a plan for how you will create, distribute and monitor it for mass reach is irresponsible. The fundamentals of this strategy need to ascertain what you're doing, pick a trajectory that honors the people your message serves, define your own levels of success, and value understanding more than it values being judgemental. Whether it's a new album or a social action campaign, intention and impact are very different things. Intention without action items rarely yields the desired results.

It's very easy to find books and blogs that outline media strategy step by step, so here's what is seldom microscoped about the process. *Sustaining a media strategy* and creating a *sustainable media strategy* are different. In the sustaining scenario, the plan simply reacts, chases or coasts until it eventually hits a wall, falls off or fades. A sustainable approach stays mutable as needed and while having clear objectives, it doesn't maintain rigidity for rigidity's sake. It's willing to play, which means you can take risks while also having fun. Protection isn't deprioritized. Layers of offense and defense are still built in. Yet, the plan's center requires hope and joy or it will be overtaken by fear and hyper-reaction. The group that serves as stewards for this strategy must desire to amplify the joy over the danger, or they might get burnt out and broken down.

Joy within the process of media outreach is often found within a strong team that is passionate, capable, and therefore, able to seize opportunities as they magically appear. Think of these three elements — passion, ability, and opportunity — as chances at success and where they overlap, prosperous metrics abound. Of course, plans can also be devised and implemented via strictly solo efforts. They just tend to be less daunting and more fun when a group of motivated people with diverse skill sets are working together toward a common vision.

So of course, stating an **actionable goal** is where we begin. Vague ideas will lead to vague paths and very vague results. Make up your mind about 1 to 3 things that need to happen when you reach out to media, create content, distribute and energize your community. This is a north star for the endeavor.

This actionable goal should harmonize with your clear **proposition statement**. It's where you easily, effectively state the problem or situation and what your fresh solution is. The proposition should be flexible and so that it can be malleable over time as the team finds more data or makes more progress towards attaining the envisioned achievement.

Research should stay a part of the process because it helps you better understand the community you serve, the overall stakeholders and the folks that oppose your message. I'm not referring to hard data, per se. The anecdotal is usually where the real issues in life emerge lightyears before scientific evidence exists to quantify it. Knowing these narratives requires talking to the community and getting to the emotional heart of what's really happening with people.

Understanding these stories can help you better understand what went right and what went wrong with previous, similar efforts. It will help you purposefully analyze collaborations and competing campaigns. It will aid your context mapping as you see what's going on in real-time in relation to your media strategy. Ultimately, it helps you see where your core passion and core beliefs align with the human needs of your target community so that you can better serve them.

The actionable goal, proposition statement and research will help clarify your media objectives. Your approach should be SMART:

Specific: clean and clear

Metrics: measurable goals and results

Achievable: actually feasible for the team and support base

Realistic: moving toward a real, tangible outcome

Timely/Timeless: on the pulse of an urgent need and evergreen in its human truths wherever possible

Keeping these objectives in mind is what can help your media not just relate, but resonate. It hits people where they live. It applies to the very context of the culture.

The media that you create and distribute is usually going to amplify one of 4 things: diversity, inclusivity, belonging, or equity. While this language often defines cultural movements, all these terms have real life equivalency.

Diversity is a fact of life on planet Earth. The world is naturally diverse. Inclusivity is a conscious action of a society or system. A system has to make an effort to be inclusive because exclusivity always exists somewhere. Belonging is a cure for "aloneness" but can also be a trick. While we need a sense of belonging, it can come with individual compromise in order to "fit in." When people are scared of being excluded, they will settle for a compromised sense of belonging because they know equity is not an actual option. Equity is the real end goal, for this reason and many others. Equity allows people to exist without fear of exclusion because they have equitable stake in the systems on which they depend. It bypasses the anxieties of being existentially alone by offering a possible self determination and actualization within the system of life.

Being mindful of these distinctions and people's desires around them informs how your media is SMART. It helps you decide when to raise awareness and where to create calls to action. It allows you to pinpoint when community-generated content is needed and helps you ask correctly for the stories and videos you must curate directly from the community. If you get really smart, this knowledge can help you shape a message and media strategy that avoids shame and blame by getting to the heart of accountability.

It even offers you insight into what will compel compassionate response, how to energize ambassadors and stakeholders, and in what ways to adjust your proposition statement to stay on the pulse. These are the key elements that will align with your core message, your outreach to allies and collaborations, the offense and defense you build around your narrative, and how you continue to read culture as it shifts.

This is a lot of strategy. For sanity's sake, surrender is needed, too. Surrender isn't where you lie down and give up. It's acknowledgment of the inability to achieve perfection. Something will always fall through the cracks. You can craft a succinct, sublime 25-point plan and someone will hate the entire thing because of the font used to type it up. Maybe your font choice was splendorous. Maybe it wasn't well thought through. Maybe you enlisted the wrong graphic designer. Get over your ego and adjust the plan wherever it makes sense to do so without compromising its core intention.

Our minds are opened when comfort is offered to the disrupted and disruption is offered to the comfortable. If your media strategy seeks to repair what is inequitable, then you must equally embrace the areas of harmony and disharmony. You're challenging round-heeled thought. You're making us notice what has gone unnoticed or unspoken. You're calling out betrayal so that we can heal it. This type of action makes it impossible to people-please across the board but it insists on a ton of mutability in real-time. So develop a team that can handle this with real vision and resiliency.

Our sense of individuality treats thinking as if it's a solo effort. But *thought improves* when understanding expands.

THINKING *is a* COLLABORATIVE PROCESS.

Our range of thinking is always defined by what we don't know, what we don't notice and what we fail to acknowledge. We need each other's perspectives.

13

Perspective × Perception

How do you know if your perception is rooted in deception? If you've built your entire life philosophy on an illusion of certainty, it's even harder to know how much the deception has actually affected you. We like to think that storytellers shape the stories, but it's usually the opposite. Few of us question the origins of the stories we tell ourselves or why we believe certain frameworks to be true of society and systems. It's extraordinarily easy to discount our understanding of the world through our senses when we get contradictory narratives from our culture and subsequent media culture.

We all inherit multiple cultural legacies at once. Culture is a floating world hovering over everything, often unseen. Each of us live in a psycho-socio-cultural cosmos that determines norms as insouciantly as it influences passing trends. There are layers upon layers of it specific to:

- where you were born

- when you were born
- to whom you were born
- how you were born
- what body you were born into
- what you encounter as you grow
- who you encounter as you encounter these things

Add to that how your society plays out around all these numerous variables, and it becomes clear that culture is as much a personal experience as it is a group phenomena.

Culture is the colonizer, manipulator, liberator, equalizer, ambassador and guru. It seamlessly weaves its way through our lives while shaping the stories we tell and the stories we believe. It turns ordinary people into larger-than-life legends. It obliterates entire dynasties from history. It often determines whether you were raised to think of yourself as an individual or part of a collective. So, it can even shape the way you build relationships, collaborations, conflicts, competitions and compromises, your entire life. All these different cultural wavelengths determine what is relevant/significant and what is trending or trusted at any given moment.

The umbrella over all of these cultural subelements is our overarching human culture. Our collective culture has always existed but only a few people have ever had enough reach and influence to tap it. In the past, this level of ubiquity was reserved for certain inventors, world leaders, entertainers, philosophers, scientists and scholars deemed by academics and educators to be chosen and highly influential.

Tech and media have now made ubiquity possible for almost

anyone. The interconnectedness is also helping us realize that we are more alike than different; we're now acutely aware of how much time we all spend seeking. What we seek varies but the activity of search is universal.

We've explored every inch of land on this planet. We fly at will. We've even gotten into space. We're planning to colonize Mars. It can seem, few mysteries are left. But consider how much we still don't know about our own planet. The ocean covers 70 percent of the Earth, but we've only explored 5 percent of it. Combine that with infinite space and there's still more questions than answers.

Perhaps culture confounds us even more than space and the oceans. It's uniquely an environment that exists within us and outside of us, daily shaping how we interpret life itself. The ways in which these systems, behaviors and symbols are expressed in our narratives can make us limited or limitless. How these messages consistently change over time is how culture itself changes.

Our narratives are more relevant than ever. Modern life is hectic, busy, distracting, stressful and complex. The more complex things get, the more we need and seek storylines that help us find simplicity. As technology helps us better feel some sort of mastery over our world, we also grow more aware of the lack of mastery we sense over ourselves.

In this context, we don't just use media for entertainment, communication or promotion. We also need it for gathering data that will help us make quick decisions so we can keep going on about our demanding lives. For this reason, almost every culture is making some form of media. Our connectivity is increasing daily and, for the first time ever, we're forming a true collective human culture, whether some of us like it or not.

Folks are getting fed up about the same things at the same time. Ideas spread through memes. Folks are galvanizing around collaborative notions of wellbeing and purposeful pursuits. Tribalism is forming around anti-tribes, meaning that we're grouping based on what we hate together rather than what we believe in or for that which we aim.

Media culture is helping drive this. Being able to access each other's stories and experiences while sharing our views and situations is showing us we're more alike than we think. It's also highlighting how much advantage we gain in our complexity and abilities to think together. Yet, the media has also amplified the divisions.

Algorithms can steer what we see but… that's true of everything in life. The words we use to describe things in the physical world often behave like algorithms, only pointing us in the direction that we describe, only showing us results based on the vocabulary we use to navigate our search. You often won't find the information you don't seek. You get lucky to find the information you didn't know to seek.

There are many people hoping to change the minds of other people and, therefore, change an entire system of thought, practices and policies. Such a shift rarely happens quickly. It typically takes many decades for a generation to fully embrace new possibilities. Just look at U.S. history. The abolitionist movement took 40 years from the 1830s to 1870. The woman suffrage movement began in 1848 and in 1920 only white women won the right to vote. The civil rights movement took place between the 1950s and 60s but was imperative due to 73 years of legally enforced racial inequity.

The slow math of shift is the case for cultural legacy. Progress usually requires vision that can last at least three generations, if not longer. It has to gain amplifiers and ambassadors to further the message after the initial visionary, that fountainhead of wonderment, is dead. It holds a promise that people pursue for decades, offers answers for our search toward a better life and always lives somewhere within media culture.

Where legacies get exhausted is where too much core mentality abounds. The foundational energy of the legacy is in preaching to the converted through like-minded media outlets and pundits. The shifting energy is in the good-natured people who don't know at all, don't know enough or don't know why they should care more. It's in moving the comfortable towards compassionate action. The message has to find people who have never wondered about the solution because they're too comfortable to notice the deep problem let alone ask why. It has to cause them disharmony in order to demand repair (and reparations) that moves towards a better harmony.

If your media strategy gets stuck in silos and only talks to those who already agree, it is sustaining but it isn't sustainable. It is not appreciated the illusion of certainty and the human need to be relieved of that. It isn't taking into account our collective need to seek. It's not even noticing how individualized culture has shifted beyond just the need for belonging to also demand the space to become. We think people hate change, and that's true. People also crave change. Both are true. We're ambivalent, sentient, social creatures.

This is why the sublime wonder within a cultural legacy is not just a safe space of comfort for the disrupted. At it's best, it is also a safe uncomfortable space for the comfortable to become disrupted. Here, this individual can finally ask a question in their own mind, and that question's very existence will leave them disquieted and chaotic until they also find the answer. Both energies, the disrupted and the disrupting, are necessary for growth and vigor. For how does a congregation grow if it doesn't pursue and welcome new converts?

14

Cultural Legacy As Trajectory

Cultural legacy is knowledge, skills and ideologies passed down to us from previous generations through which we find our perspective about ourselves, our world, our cosmos, our very existence and our place within the system of life. Without cultural legacy, we have no initial view of reality and therefore no starting point on the roadmap we will charter for our individual lives. It includes interactions with status and class, opportunity and trauma, economic systems and social constructs that expand or restrict one's reach.

Cultural legacy helps us choose paths, pick lanes and shape our personal beliefs, which in turn shape our identities and authenticities, what we believe is possible for ourselves, what we believe is possible for our world, what we accept and what we aspire towards.

It's a combination of behaviors, environment and norms that define and message daily life. It's where ritual exists and where ritual is devoid. Cultural legacy embodies the ways we strive to turn all this chaos into context. It combines sacred simplicity with sacred complexity.

We all contribute to it in different ways. So, what do you hope your cultural legacy will be? What is it you wish to contribute? What is the song in your heart and why do you feel compelled to sing it? Where should it be bold and grand? Where does it need to be made into bite-size pieces for easier transport to others? What already exists in the media landscape that can be used as tools and pathways?

15

Our Needs. Our Cultures.

A lot of our culture developed in an effort to help us with angst. We're constantly trying to reconcile two schools of thought: life is beautiful versus the world is shit. Generations before have brought forth ideas of purpose, morality interwoven into religious dogma and even the idea that we chose to be here. At the end of the day, we have no concrete evidence of anything, only hunches here and there that help us deal. The fact that we observe bright blue skies alongside cold hard facts of child molestation, agents of change alongside human traffickers and the sublime juxtaposed with utter sadism doesn't somehow stop us from yearning for and striving toward wonder. Within that battle worn, battle scarred optimism is in fact the wonder itself. Where there is mystery, confusion and wonder, there is cultural legacy.

Being alive comes with so much freaking angst. The weird thing is that we need the angst, but we seldom appreciate its magical qualities since, often, we experience too much angst. So our culture and narratives help us escape from it, if only for the length of a meditation or an action movie.

Our minds are under siege with chatter. This makes us believe the breaks from the angst are more valuable than the actual angst. We see more value in the pleasures and luxuries that help us escape all these bombarding thoughts that seem to be holding us back from our potential and happiness.

According to scientist Daniel Kahneman, most people experience at least 20,000 thoughts a day, and 600,000 per month. That's a lot of processing when you consider that the human brain only holds about 1.7GB of information.

Thoughts rule. But thoughts are different from your actual voice. Your voice is connected to your truth and inner joy. Your voice is most interested in your wellbeing: your passion, mission, actions and thriving. Culture tries to help us make sense of all the thoughts and find a peace with them. Ideally, our cultural legacies are trying to help us cut through the noise so we can stay true to the inner voice, instinct and talent that will help us succeed.

The first step toward using media to build your cultural legacy is to be knowledge, not noise. You have to start with you. Cultural legacy is constructed through storytelling that weaves into the cultural ideology. To build such a thing, you have to declare your convictions.

16

Owning It: Conviction

The easiest way to define your convictions: if when confronted with a person, place or thing perceived as more powerful than you, if your conviction immediately dissolves, shifts and becomes irrelevant, it probably isn't your actual conviction. Your true convictions are non-negotiable. Your viewpoint might evolve as you gain more insight, but it doesn't coward before power.

Your non-negotiables help you craft your perspective. Perspectives and opinions aren't the same thing. Anyone can have an opinion, or perception, about anything. Perspective stems from insider information, digging in the dirt and living with an actual viewpoint.

Own your perspective, then disrupt the perception around such perspective. Originality of topic isn't necessary. The original part is you, your unique take, your unique style and your unique content.

There's pressure to be likable. Don't be too weird or unruly. Appear malleable enough for other people to project upon you.

Any strategy that isn't you is a losing strategy. True legends step into their truth and stand out. People get worried about being seen in a bad light, but it's never a bad angle to be seen as a person of principle. And you can't have principle without perspective. Your specificity matters.

17

Disrupting or Disrupted?

Choose a perspective then, disrupt the perceptions of that perspective. Thinking like everyone else and talking like everyone else doesn't break through the noise. It blends. In this world, it usually boils down to whether you are disrupting or being disrupted. Ignoring your perspective to go with the flow is the actuality of being disrupted.

Even the Goliath of media has grand structure. It has rules, order and edicts that we take for granted. It's organized to tap our senses. Tropes, motifs and archetypes abound within the narratives that media transmits so that they can resonate and find purpose within us. The system is funds and demands funds as well as human capital, the individual's energy to house the message and forward the narrative to others.

So you must begin with your perspective. Your core passion and core beliefs will determine your intentions and vocabulary. Where they overlap is where you will find your target audience and community.

Look at all the tropes around your idea. The tropes exist

because they're already funded. You can use them as tethers or deliberate contrasts to your message. Find the current perceptions and then disrupt them with your specific perspective. This action is what will expand the perspectives of others and that expansion will feel like wonderment.

This visceral sublime is the lifeblood of the legacy. It keeps it energized. It helps it stay clear and clean. The life force helps you know what to repeat, how to present the message, how to keep redistributing it. It gives the process buoyancy. It encourages others to support it and provide communal lift. It can help you build an ecosystem of capital; resources you can consistently build and tap to keep fueling growth and options.

Building from your unique experience and perspective gives you tactical advantage amongst monotony and people pleasers. It helps craft that signature style and public image that can provide funding for the legacy. Actors become lauded and memorable because of what they uniquely bring to roles and the craft. This is true of everyone in every endeavor.

There's nothing wrong with being a cover band, unless you want to play your own, original music. If you're building your cultural legacy then you have to express your narrative through your insight. That's what your community is going to be seeking from you.

People want to know who you are so that they can better understand what you can do for them. This doesn't make people lecherous user trash bags. It's perfectly normal to want to understand someone else's significance in relation to our own needs for information, health, survival and so on.

Originality of topic isn't necessary. You want to tap what's topical and relevant. So, you need to connect with concepts already in the zeitgeist.

Your goal isn't to expose people to new things that they can't wrap their heads around. You need to help people see the things they can't wrap their heads around in new ways. Turn all the confusion into connections. Help people find the simplicity they seek through what you're contributing.

The media is a stream. Septillions of dollars have been invested into it, ensuring it flows in many directions. The system is pristine and designed to be used to make money, not just spread information. As George Lipsitz states, "The stories that sell are the stories they tell." But as Dr. Nicole Haggard iterates, "This also means that the stories that sold are the ones that keep getting told." The media system supports old and emerging narrative tropes. Once you own your perspective, you can determine which tropes vibe with your viewpoint and use them to propel your cultural contribution.

Like being in running water, there are options. You can swim up and against the current. This will require lots of funds and resources. You can get caught up in the stream, get swept away and be lost. You can even go with the flow to move faster and expend less energy.

You can also redirect the stream. This is one of my favorite options and my ideal way to do it is to carve a sub-niche and then utilize the energy already flowing toward the overarching niche. Nothing slows down. It just finds new direction. This takes time. You have to build up a combination of resources, community and momentum.

This is the idea. Examine all that is popular. Distinguish the noise around it from what you truly believe and make it your own rather than just being made by it. From this, you will shape every aspect of your messaging, content and publicity strategies. It helps you get past your myriad thoughts and find your actual voice. Tapping into your inner voice that is unclouded by fear, confusion and obligation will help you set your intentions. It will fuel your momentum.

Infusing your message with your story is a requirement. This isn't optional. Prepare to practically get nauseous from how much you have to repeat yourself. This is why you must believe in the words pouring from your mouth and you must make your inner speak align with your motivations and intentions. You will speak worlds with your words and what you say will either deplete you or empower you. If you don't believe, the wear and tear will break you.

Once you're speaking with conviction, you'll still need to challenge your creativity. To avoid burnout, find fresh ways to talk about your journey. Explore visuals, immersive storytelling and other narrative arts. Yet, none of this will negate the fact that you will have to tell your story over and over, to the same groups and different groups. You will share it until you know it forwards and backwards. If you're lucky, just when you think you know all there is to know about your journey and your viewpoints, you'll discover something new.

Within your specificity is the universality. Tell your perspective. Share your experience. Your narrative won't just relate. It will resonate.

18

Capital As Self-Efficacy

Stretch your parameters regarding wealth. Let this be an ever-expanding construct. The goal is to find abundance where others see lack ad resources where most only observe deficit. Wealth is:

1. **Time:** your actual hours you have to exist, work and play
2. **Physical:** your physical body's ability to produce and help you make money through health and stamina
3. **Emotional:** your understanding of your emotions and the emotional states of others
4. **Financial:** your monetary resources
5. **Social:** your access to different types of people, your network reach and the resources of your social circles
6. **Content:** your insight and creativity crafted into workable, reworkable, monetizable and distributable media
7. **Distribution:** your ability to disseminate your information and products

8. **Data:** your access to quality facts and statistics
9. **Information:** your access to quality sequencing of viable facts
10. **Knowledge:** your access to insightful facts, information, skills and experience
11. **Wisdom:** your ability to use knowledge for unbiased thinking and action through a combination of compassion, experiential self-awareness and the deep questioning of rigidity.

Your attitude while building all the forms of your wealth will inform your legacy and media strategy regarding it. You will build what you believe. If you look in the mirror and see abundance, the energy of abundance will be placed into your strategy. You will see opportunity where others find lack. You'll pursue harmony and repair where others only see disharmony. You'll better appreciate where you need to rest and replenish and better understand how to reach out to your community for additional fuel.

Realize that with care and dedication, every category can become your asset. There's something unburdening about knowing you have means. I'm referring to having means within yourself as well as externally. Appreciating your own knowledge and respecting your own time is just as valuable as having money, support, and confidants. So throughout your journey, ask for what you're worth because some folks will deliberately undercut you and still expect you to say "thanks" when they do it. Ask for what you're worth so that you can continue to give the legacy what it needs to be sustainable.

Seeing and welcoming abundance is the first step into deeper, more nourishing self compassion. The more you understand the nectar of being kind to yourself, the more it will become clear that self compassion isn't a passive state of being. It demands action.

19

Find the Source of Your Energy

EXERCISE #2
GET TO THE CORE.

We don't build what we don't believe. Our endeavors always begin within. Everything is a guessing game and the only difference lies in whether our guesses are educated or pure hunch. The only real compass you'll find along the way is your intention and intuition. That's why it's important to employ strategy wherever possible. The first place is in figuring out what to create.

QUESTION 1: What is your core passion? What is the thing you're most passionate about that you believe suits your talent and is the element in which you thrive? This can be music, writing, acting, beauty product, makeup artistry, illustration... you get it.

QUESTION 2: What are your top 3 core beliefs? These are the beliefs you have about your passion, and possibly life itself. For instance, your top 3 beliefs about illustration can be 1. Practice 2. Patience 3. Resilience. These can also be aspects about life: practice is the key to self growth, patience with yourself is crucial, resilience is required to learn.

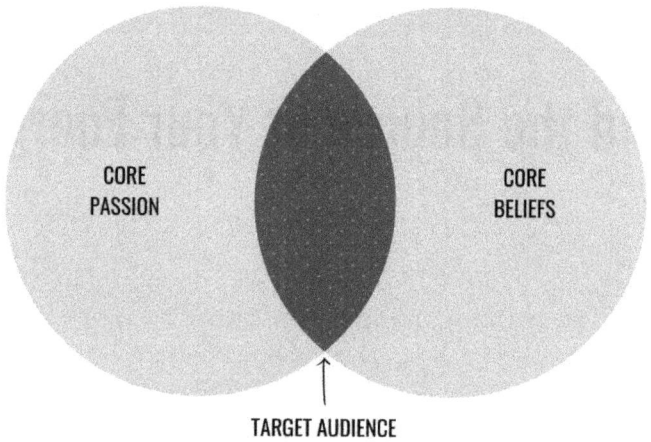

Where your Cores merge is where you'll find your target community. The audience you seek is seeking someone who focuses on your core passion and demystifies the 3 areas, or core beliefs, you view as central to success in the specific pursuit. This is how they'll get to know who you are and get an idea of what you can do for them. Your goal is to create content for each of these core beliefs that fully honors your core passion. You must do this in your unique style, through your disruptive perspective.

QUESTION 3: What is your unique style? This is where you get to show off your skills and personality. This is the display that not only attracts community, but also business opportunities. *There's nothing new to say, so the difference is you choosing your perspective and voicing it through your unique experiences.*

There's no need to develop a personae. Your actual personality is the key to distinguishing yourself. Make sure that every message you send out is in your voice, true to your style and core beliefs. If it doesn't align, don't publish it.

QUESTION 4: What does your community seek from you? People want to know who you are so that they can understand what you can do for them.

20

What the Ancestors Knew

You've gotta hand it to the ancients, they understood the power of storytelling. They knew that imagination, morality, standards, identity and talent could be groomed anecdotally. They also understood pathos, a narrative's ability to evoke sadness and pity for a character. They figured out that if a narrative keeps getting repeated, the audience eventually feels personally connected to this character and vested in their story, thereby letting that protagonist be seen more deeply as a hero figure worthy of compassion and championship. Repetition calms the need to question and it welcomes acceptance. Our need for stories seems built in. It's how we understand, plan and implement.

There's a Kenyan proverb that states, "Until lions start writing down their own stories, the hunters will always be the heroes." Our ancestors may not have verbalized it this way, but they fundamentally understood that storytelling begins with perspective. They realized that learning stories is how you study culture, but changing stories is how culture shifts.

This is why representation matters. It's important to make sure certain groups are seen and given platforms for voice. Without a storyline in life's vast melodrama, these groups have a hard time finding connection and empathy within mainstream thought. They don't get rooted for or championed. The zeitgeist can disregard their journey and hardships as sentimentality, over exaggerations or a ploy to gain some sort of advantage that's underhanded.

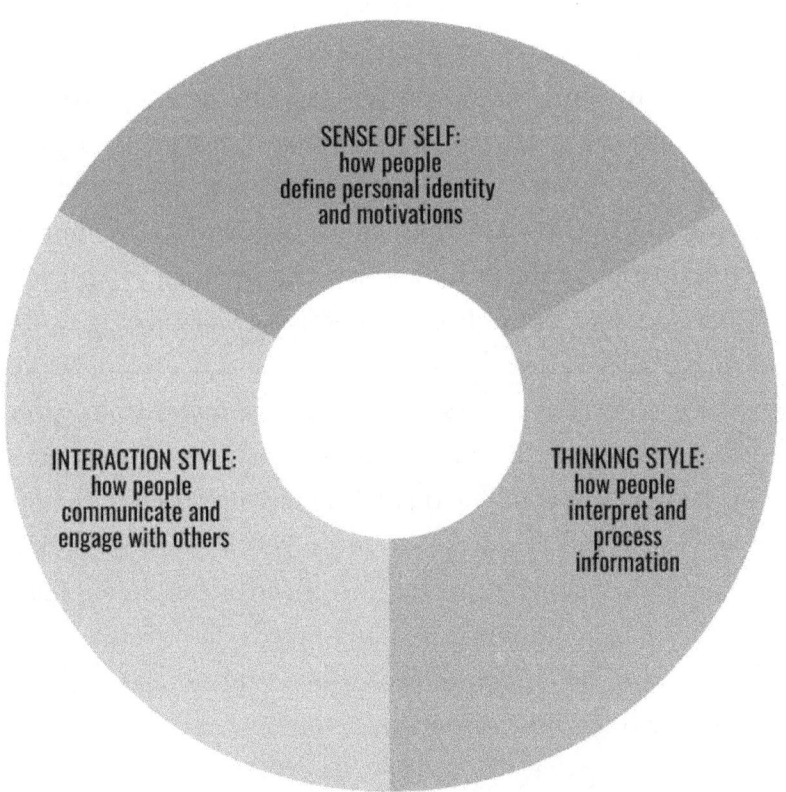

In learning and acceptance, repetition is key. We don't just tell a child one time, "A, B, C, D, ... got it, kid? Great. Good luck." We create alphabet songs, alphabet games, alphabet cards, building blocks with letters on them and any other type of avatar for the lesson possible. The child's entire environment is in cahoots to make certain the knowledge is embedded.

Our ancestors also understood that stories shaped societal behaviors and the tropes we use to reinforce them. Our sense of self, thinking style and interaction style are intermingled with and influenced by our cultural beliefs. These aspects of our separate and collaborative thinking also get reworked by written language and, therein, written stories.

Reading and written language rewires our brains. Not only does it create more white matter and aid memory. Reading actively shifts attitudes toward the subject matter by inviting empathy for the central characters of a story. Novel and biography reading in particular is an opportunity to immerse your imagination in the life of another and live their experience.

While you read, not only do you hear the words being read in your mind, but you (usually) specifically hear those words in your own voice. Your larynx and throat muscles involved in speech actually contract as if you are speaking aloud. That alone is trippy. So now let's combine that with more neuroscience.

Broca's area and Wernicke's area are classic language regions, but scientists are finding that narratives activate even more parts of the brain. For instance, reading words like "lavender" or "coffee" ignite the language-processing centers and olfactory cortex of the brain simultaneously.

We're learning that the news media doesn't generally have the same effect. News can go ignored when people don't have a fundamental basis to care. Our narrative arts don't need virtual or augmented reality to be immersive. The empathy they spark makes them naturally absorbing.

Empathy is what lets a documentary be as enrapturing as a group discussion or coming-of-age novel grow a fanbase eager to see a big screen adaptation. Empathy is the storytelling. Storytelling is shared experience. Shared experience is walking in someone else's shoes and growing from their journey.

Every lesson our ancestors put into proverbs, they also include in folklore, story and myth. We've been turning these lessons into novels, film and television ever since. Which means we've also been perfected these art forms with compassion-infused arcs. Storytelling has been used as a blueprint and a mindset. Yet, when it's examined for empathy, it takes on a much deeper meaning.

Andrew Jackson was the seventh president of the United States and an example of using media to build notable empathy. He became known as the Great Expansionist because he gained more land for the country by signing the Indian Removal Act of 1830. This led to the Trail of Tears in 1838: 16,000 Native Americans were forcibly marched across 1200 miles of difficult terrain until they were relocated on less desirable land. 4,000 indigenous people died of famine and disease during the journey. Andrew Jackson died at the age of 78 and eventually got his face on the $20 bill.

Before taking presidential office, Jackson garnered the reputation of war hero for defeating the British in the Battle of New Orleans during the War of 1812. Here's the part that fascinates me.

Jackson didn't leave it up to fate or chance for the country to view him as a hero. He hired three biographers to write his story and distribute it. Some people read his story. Others had it read and performed for them, but the results were the same.

He used the narrative arts to promote himself, and that status helped him become electable. It also helped him gain empathy. American history books pedestalize his expansionism, but during his time, he was known as the "people's president" and respected for being self-made — which is a triumphant *rags to riches* trope America always loves. It helped him be revered for his journey.

Few Americans rarely think of him for the Trail of Tears. Even fewer know that he owned 150 slaves and if one escaped, he would offer "ten dollars, for every 100 lashes any person will give him [the enslaved escapee], to the amount of three hundred." Such an order was essentially a death sentence. Jackson's cruelty is long forgotten. Instead, he's money. That's how well he solidified his narrative and the country's cultural legacy has followed suit.

Our current environment has a lot of noise that seems to be the by-product of a post-truth, artifice-ridden world. Empathy through storytelling breaks through all of that. So, your cultural legacy requires storytelling through the narrative arts. Each society has certain tropes that are loved and perpetuated to the point of being unnoticed while they remain highly influential.

Brand building idealism focuses on news media, but cultural legacy building requires using the narrative arts in conjunction with all media. News media is great for spreading information, but the narrative arts inspire empathy. That means the feature on your local news is great, but it won't create the deep connections that your memoir, docuseries or even a film based on your journey will yield. Storytelling that deep dives and shows the various ugly and beautiful aspects of your human experience makes your legacy relatable and beloved.

Yet, not all empathy is the same. When your story can evoke the most powerful form of this emotion, it can inspire real change that adheres to your philosophy.

21

Not All Empathy Is Equal

I remember imagining the possibility of fairies, or any form of magic, within that night. Even though I'd known since the age of 5 that fairies were fiction, at 7 years old I had a brief moment where I fantasized I would hold witness to wonder...

You see, my family had just moved across town into a middle-class suburb of Macon, Georgia. We were the first black family in our neighborhood. It was the 80's. Ronald Reagan was president. Shoulder pads were in everything, even t shirts.

There was newness in my world. I loved my big, new bedroom. I was anxious about my new school and hoped I'd make new friends. Some of our immediate neighbors rang the doorbell to say hi and drop off fresh baked cookies. Despite my change of environment, I was discovering that most of my daily life felt the same, but also different.

One night, I'm lying in bed, very successfully staying wide awake. I see a warm golden glow outside my window and start imagining it as Christmas lights. This, however, makes no sense because it's July, so, I expand and dream up fairies. I remember parting the blinds with my little fingers, ready to behold something otherworldly. As the blinds separate, I see a huge cross burning on the parcel of lawn outside my bedroom window — it is the source of what I'd hoped was fairy magic.

Now, I hear my mom yelling. My is dad running outside with a hose to extinguish the flames. My big brother emerges from the ether of that trauma and snatches me from the window, but it's too late. I will never unsee that cross.

At 7, I hadn't experienced racism let alone racial terror. Over the next several days, weeks and months, my family slowly reveals to me the story of my country and how it has treated people born into black bodies like mine. My parents then explain that they grew up in North Carolina during Jim Crow, a system of legalized segregation that kept black Americans in second class citizen status. They explain Martin Luther King, Jr., Malcolm X and Rosa Parks.

I absorb. It's heartbreaking, but having never known the struggle, I had no real point of reference for it. None of this new information negated the primary issue. What gave these people the right to mess with my family? We hadn't done anything to anyone.

As I listen to my parents, I just find that I'm completely pissed off. In fact, I believe my anger saved me. That I had, at such a young age, experienced my life in a way where I felt the right to be angry when dealt such overt inhumanity seemed like my moment of becoming. That I had the inner life to hold that anger and use it as creative fuel while I imagined my future self unstoppably existing above that moment felt like a divine spark of defiance. Right then and there, I start making declarations to myself about the kind of person I will be and the life I will lead.

My folks, the sheriff and our Sicilian neighbor across the street got in cahoots to do a coordinated neighborhood watch and even had a deputy staked out in our neighbor's driveway. Their teamwork eventually put a stop to what was a series of attacks to our property. In the end, it wasn't even grown people enacting most of these terrors; they were being masterminded and implemented by the teenage sons and daughters of our neighbors. We can only imagine what series of events in their own lives led them to believe their actions would be a great use of their time on this planet.

Once it was all over, my family never talked about it. We survived it. We moved past it.

35 years later, in 2018, I joined a cohort called *50WomenCan* that is dedicated to achieving gender parity within media and entertainment. We met Gayle Guest Brown, a leadership coach, who came to guest lecture. Gayle had us break into small groups and share our family stories in order to tap deeper levels of our natural leadership abilities.

I didn't really know what I was going to share, but I walked into that room 100 percent certain I wouldn't go to that moment at my bedroom window. Yet, when it was my turn, my Judas tongue started spilling it all. For the first time, and within a mixed group of women, I talked out loud about that ugly moment in my life. Many cried, including me. One of my cohort sisters leapt from her seat and held me while we both wept. It was a vulnerable, empowering experience that hit me completely by surprise.

While no one else had walked my exact journey, everybody was moved by the frightening thought of being attacked or terrorized for no reason other than who they naturally are. The thought was so connective that one person was compelled to jump from her chair and physically embrace me.

It's not performance art. Within our specificity is the universality. Although that night all those years ago didn't reveal fairy magic, the power our stories have to connect us has helped me hold witness to wonder. That wondrous thing has multiple levels.

There are 3 fundamental layers of connective feeling for someone else's plight: **sympathy**, **empathy** and **compassion**. Sympathy simply feels something, usually you feel bad for the person. Sometimes this could be classified as pity. Empathy tries to understand. But compassion compels you to do what you can to ease another's suffering — you stand up, speak up, rally around, donate, organize or volunteer. Compassion is a requisite for action.

I've learned to never underestimate a human's ability for immense compassion and generosity of spirit. I've also learned to never underestimate a human's ability for immense indifference and disregard. When building outreach, it's best to keep both of these possibilities in mind.

Simply having your story told creates empathy and empathy will help people relate to your cultural legacy. Compassion is much deeper. Empathy strives to understand and the more mysterious someone's story is, the more questions people ask attempting to understand. It's almost a puzzle.

Compassion happens once a person believes they understand enough to jump to action. It reinforces a human entanglement that helps us think in a collaborative process. Picture someone choking in a restaurant. This person isn't making speaking or yelling for help because they're choking and can't talk. Yet, somehow, you can look at them and understand they need help clearing their throat. If you know the Heimlich maneuver, you'll rush over to them and perform it. If you don't, you might yell for a doctor and declare, "They're choking!"

The magic of compassion sidesteps a lot of back and forth because it already sees and understands the human issue at the heart. It helps us connect and interconnect. It allows us to expose vulnerable moments with strength and resolve because the ego becomes less important than the vision. We lean into what is bigger than our individual selves.

When people are going through something similar, their shared experience almost feels like synchronized movement. That synchronicity gets promoted in the body by a rise in oxytocin, the "love" hormone that bonds mothers to their babies, helps lovers feel like soul mates, and connects groups in camaraderie. Appreciating this provides a framework for your storytelling talents.

Communicating experience in the right spaces and places can widen the narrative landscape around an entire idea. This can inspire people to either embrace or investigate a well-traveled trope. It invites your community to journey with you into a new understanding of what we think we already know.

22

All These Tropes

Encouraging compassion through storytelling and media is a multi-pronged process. It requires bringing forth a part of the message that is tethered to human saga. Identity groups rely on tropes. Whether it be a country, a political party or even a religion, there are sagas that transmit values, life lessons, and the characteristics of heroes versus villains. Take America's political sagas, for example. As explained by political commentator, Robert Reich, the nation's civics are typically defined by plot devices of: 1) the self-made triumphant hero, 2) the good-natured community, 3) the threatening mob, and 4) the rot at the top.

America has always been a politicized entity founded in rebellion from the monarchy and taxation without representation. The founding fathers were visionary philosophers who declared independence and rights to pursue their own happiness while also colonizing indigenous lands and enslaving populations of people. However, many of them promoted personal stories of being triumphant individual successes who made careers attacking the rot at the top. Their ideas of *the villains* were always prominently promoted and this mentality is present in most American storytelling whether it be politics, young adult fiction, or a feature film.

Precise compassionate storytelling can rally the passionate support. The easiest, and often laziest way, to send out a unifying battle cry is with a narrative that exposes the **villain** as either:

1. **the rot**
2. **the mob**

Let's return for a moment to that burning cross outside my bedroom window. Within a narrative, this harrassment is the mob at the gates. The coalition of my parents and big brother, the sheriff and our neighbor becomes the benevolent community. Since this is my story, I get to be the triumphant individual. Voila. That's how seamless it is to apply a ubiquitous trope.

These tropes engulf daily life and play out around us. Different cultures have different tropes, but America's political tropes also tie in to ideas of the hero's journey of Greek and Roman mythologies that Anglo-Saxon cultures carried to North America. The United States is obsessed with hero tropes and hard lines of good versus evil.

Other countries have their own preoccupations. Japan leans into the samurai and Bushido. England loves knights and medieval times. Nigeria often tackles co-wife tropes laced with animosity.

I once polled filmmakers on Twitter about tropes they were

tired of seeing in film. The main ones that came up were:

white savior, magical negro, able bodied person faking disability, sassy ethnic female nurse or receptionist, trickster bisexual or trans person.

As this quick and very unscientific poll illustrates, some tropes disappoint some of us. Some tropes are attached to archetypes and others are attached to stereotypes. Tropes aren't evil, but the ways they get used can either be beneficial or completely farted out. Disruptors and change agents seek to throw away the tropes that no longer serve us or hit the pulse of current culture.

Regardless, we do need tropes for storytelling and narrative understanding. We can't escape them because they help us move ideas along within a story just as metaphors and analogies help us compare and contrast. This is why it's valuable to identify as many repetitive tropes as possible, and that begins with deeply understanding as many narratives as possible.

Tropes are politicized, racialized, engendered, classist, subverted, demonized and lionized in multi-tiered layers. So, with tropes in mind, let's apply the construct to the media ecosystem you're creating.

What are all the tropes connected to your narrative? Once you determine your perspective, see what vibes with it. This is a big question that warrants a detailed answer. You'll want to know all the tropes that affirm and oppose your narrative. Trace their origins, whether it be fables, historical moments, an author-coined term or a political campaign. If the origin eludes you, then understand how it is applied in other systems (like politics) and rhetoric. This is how you turn your data points into information and knowledge.

Tap into those tropes and the system of blogs, radio shows, social media pages and accounts, public events, digital podcasts, TV shows and those shows' digital platforms, and any other channels that build content along these tropes and storylines. Advertise and target their audiences. Use all the forms of paid media that make sense. Where you can, use earned media and write Op-Eds. Also advertise in all the crossover areas that your audience enjoys.

Targeted ads are the key to maintaining a pipeline into the tropes and targeted ads can shift as needed. Earned and owned media alone won't maintain the momentum without being partnered with your paid media efforts.

23

Pioneering Is the Best Life Ever?

Sometimes, you're the first to do something in a big way and your approach changes everything. This is great positioning, but you don't want to be alone. If what you're doing is truly special, it's going to inspire others to become your peers. As peers and admirers jump on board to amplify the idea with more content and marketing, momentum grows. Momentum attracts momentum. That's when pioneering goes well but what happens when it becomes insular is another story.

Exceptionalism can make you a target among your peers. Especially if you make them all look bad. Some people won't know how to separate their aspirations from their frustrations, so they'll be jealous of you when in actuality, they're just ambitious and they know they want to accomplish more.

In general, people are more open to pioneers than they are prophets. Prophets can feel too otherworldly. Pioneers are simply brave and willing to pave the road for others. Yet, either category can isolate you and too much isolation will stunt your growth.

I don't believe power corrupts. It's isolation that corrupts us. You were born with inner power. Power is quite natural. It does not, in and of itself, corrupt. Isolation warps our minds and spirits. It manifests as tribalism that never challenges you to think beyond the group or strive for compassion. It becomes silos where you're convinced you're an island unto yourself. Isolation from accountability to others and from other's accountability to us is what corrupts. Power is natural. It doesn't twist us. It's the isolation in thought while having access to immense power that does us in. We need each other to survive. Being confined isn't natural and is often what cults and other abusers seek to do a person in order to control them.

So when you find yourself surrounded by groups who don't give you what you need to grow, you must change your environment. You must find where you're energized, not drained.

Media is one of the best ways to expand or reorganize your in-groups. Target tertiary media channels if you can't immediately access top-tier media. A niche outlet with a small but loyal, engaged audience that actively shares content is more valuable than a top-tier outlet that will provide a lot of eyeballs but not a lot of sharing. In this context, sharing and chatter is the distribution of your content and the opportunity for more business development.

Use your own social platforms to network. Reach out to strangers. Invite yourself to events. Advertise by commissioning shout outs. Guest post. Do business development that puts you into different rooms you wish to be in and you'll find your possibilities expanding through the new groups you're able to access.

24

Oxytocin As Synchrony

We still struggle to fully grasp the pursuit of happiness and how our external pleasures differ from our inner joy. This hasn't stopped us from building systems around limited understanding in the meantime. Science has identified the chemical nature of happiness and media systems have actively utilized this knowledge to gain, coax and coerce audiences, users and consumers.

The big 4 happiness chemicals go like this:

- Endorphins: reduces sense of pain
- Dopamine: increases sense of pleasure
- Serotonin: contributes to sense of satisfaction and wellbeing
- Oxytocin: contributes to sense of trust, cooperation, love and bonding

As Sue Carter, Director of the Kinsey Institute, succinctly breaks down, "Oxytocin is the secret sauce." Now linked to social bonding, this neuropeptide was long dismissed and understudied; it was largely viewed as a connecting hormone simply released between mother and child during breastfeeding or between partners during sex. Dopamine, serotonin and endorphins felt like sexier science to a lot of researchers. That research informed myriad methodologies of media and marketing in the 20th century.

Most of our current algorithms for social media are coded around dopamine responses. While dopamine helps us with feelings of pleasure, reward and motivation, it also helps us get addicted to slot machines and cocaine. Sean Parker, Napster founder and Facebook's former founding president, discussed this strategy during an Axios event in Philadelphia on November 8, 2017.

While diving into the motivation behind certain features on the Facebook platform, Parker divulges that the question for the developer team became, "How do we consume as much of your time and conscious attention as possible?" So "a little dopamine hit" was devised in the form a "like" button and "comments" in order to give encouragement for posting more to the network. Parker adds, "It's a social-validation feedback loop... exactly the kind of thing that a hacker like myself would come up with, because you're exploiting a vulnerability in human psychology."

Dopamine can get sketchy really fast. That doesn't mean that it's more vulnerable to manipulation than other chemicals. All of these happiness chemicals can be exploited. Dopamine just happens to be the most focused on, presently, because of how well it fits into concepts that use gamification. A sense of play can ignite any of the big 4. They can also all be woven into media strategy.

My personal favorite is oxytocin. I love how it works with

serotonin. When in balance, a person feels content and has more impulse control, is less prone to anxiety and depression, and feels respected by their support groups. The upside is deep bonds and secure trust-centered relationships. The downside is tribalism, betrayal blindness and the tendency toward cognitive dissonance that will keep someone attached to unhealthy, even toxic, groups when faced with facts that threaten to shatter the bond.

Like everything in this life, it's about how you use it. Boosting oxytocin within your support base, team and audience can boost empathy and compassion. Oxytocin has always helped us survive. As social creatures, we don't have a chance without bonds.

One of the most ancient flutes ever unearthed by archeologists is over 35,000 years old. That shows that music has been with us for a long time. Music serves our creativity and wellbeing, but it's also deeper than that. It helps us relate and cooperate. Playing or singing music together demands paying attention to one another, aligning in a common purpose and creatively responding to each other. Dancing on beat requires similar connection.

A 2016 study from Center for Music in the Brain (MIB) Aarhaus University/The Royal Academy of Music, Denmark found that participants given oxytocin are more synchronized when finger-tapping together. Synchronization seems to be within itself, enough to boost oxytocin and compassion. Clapping together, singing or reciting in unison and other synched movements can aid in feeling like we are more alike and similar than different.

When Piercarlo Valdesolo of Harvard University and David DeSteno of Northeastern University studied the social tuning of compassion and how it relates to synchrony, their results were straightforward. "We show that synchronous others are not only perceived to be more similar to oneself but also evoke more compassion and altruistic behavior than asynchronous others experiencing the same plight."

The experiment was easy. Two people were asked to tap rhythmically to songs for three minutes. One duo listened to the same music and found their tapping synched while the other pair listened to different songs and were out of synch. The duo that tapped in unison reported to feel:

- 26% more similar to the other person
- 20% more compassionate toward the other person

For me, this illuminates why participating in concerts, ceremonies, dance routines and rituals can be so enrapturing. The need for connection and the pathways to achieving like-mindedness are hardwired. They can be reinforced with verbal and nonverbal language, which means they can also be incorporated into messaging and media.

Let's look at Call and Response. This form of interaction is mostly associated with music — mainly jazz, blues, gospel, R&B and hip hop — religious worship and literature. The avatars of this technique differ, but the collaborative fundamentals are consistent: a phrase is put out as a call that has to be answered by some sort of response. Call and response began in sub-Saharan African cultures as a form of democratic participation. The Greeks would later witness this and incorporate it into their framework of democracy. Millennia later, call and response further developed in the Americas through enslaved work songs, field hollers (also known as field calls), spirituals and blues. It's also present in acting improv courses through exercises that employ the phrase "Yes, and" for collaborative storytelling.

Black Twitter is a bonafide field of study in the 21st century. Within the twittersphere, black users launch call and response moments often tracked through hashtags (or blacktags in this case) to joke, one up and outdo each other in clever debate or repartee. Even though these hashtag moments often take top trending spots on the social network, they're also an exclusive community building exercise in which users who understand the topic's cultural nuances create levity and camaraderie. We will often witness celebrities with ties to the black community join in the fun and reassert their relevance while also deepening peer group salience.

Like most collaborative processes, call and response builds oxytocin. It's ancient and tethered to our development of oral tradition, community building and collaborative thought.

Oxytocin building doesn't require the level of rapid fire witnessed in call and response. There are studies suggesting that oxytocin can be increased simply by using social media. It makes me consider the possibility that simply being sociable promotes the neurohormone. Making eye contact, doing mildly stressful activities in a group (such as riding roller coasters), giving gifts and sharing a meal can all foster the relaxed trusting state of mind that comes with oxytocin.

Think about how many Queen songs allow the audience to stomp their feet, clap their hands, and sing the chorus in unison with the band. They group perfected stadium rock and frontman Freddie Mercury knew how to make a massive attendance feel like they were beside him on stage. The band's Live Aid 1985 performance had a sea of 72,000 people united in synchronistic movement; that moment is regarded as one of the best live performances ever. Giving the crowd a way to participate and belong is a path toward graceful and fun-filled bond formation.

How can your content encourage this Oxytocin-building type of energy? Which media channels will best help you connect on a deeper level?

25

Popularity Is Salience

1,000 is a magic number. When one thousand people are engaged and energized around something or someone, momentum starts to feel tangible. This is more than a sizable grouping, it's a building block. Growth can begin with as little as 10 folks, but 1,000 is when everything starts to compound.

British anthropologist and evolutionary psychologist Robin Dunbar has been researching primate behavior and pair-bond relationships for decades. Although he himself doesn't know who started this term on the internet, his research is credited with Dunbar's number: a suggested cognitive limit to the amount of people with whom any one individual can maintain stable social relationships. That number, for most people, is 150.

It begins with a support clique of 3-5 people from whom you seek personal advice. It extends to a sympathy group of 12-20 with whom you make frequent contact. A band of 30-50 people are frequent acquaintances but not leaned on like the support clique. One's reach then expands to a clan of 150, a megaband of 500 and a tribe of 1,000-2,000 people that are larger social units but relatively lesser quality relationships. In the social media age, 150 seems like a frighteningly small number.

During a 2010 keynote at The RSA (Royal Society of Arts), Dunbar explained that this sizing exists for a two-fold reason. "Partly it's a cognitive challenge just to keep track of more people... The other side of it is it's a time budgeting problem." Our daily time demands — such as work, family, commuting, romantic pursuits, socializing with current relationships — make it very difficult to achieve, nurture and maintain quality connections beyond that intimate number.

It may be cruel and unusual to expect any one person to maintain tens of thousands of contacts all alone. This is why capable teams, networks, calls to action, clear objectives and salience are paramount to growth. Creating popularity is its own talent, and this layering is a path to keeping your efforts in crowded minds of others.

Popularity has its own energy. It gains or taps into a flow. Money can fund it or fuel it since the right investments can make the popularity fiscal. Popularity must be a mechanism but not the motivation. Like charisma, popularity alone is not enough to sustain anything.

Any aspect of your image, message or products that becomes popular is a wave you can comfortably ride for 3 years before you need to evolve/innovate. Not realizing this is where a lot of folks die on the hill. Nothing stays. In general, you need a community of 20,000 people who are actively and frequently engaged in a common idea or effort in order to have a full-fledged movement. By "active," I mean people who are willing to help spread the word, vouch for the effort, and possibly show up to a live event in their geographic area. By "community" I mean people you are vested in and engage directly with, not a faceless number's game audience.

20,000 is a large number made more accessible now through mailing lists, shared media, automation, and targeted ads. The real intelligence is finding that group of people, giving them energy that keeps them engaged, maintaining direct contact that has value, sourcing them for ideas and insight, and offering them delightful surprises. Again, we build large things by first thinking small. Scaling requires maintenance.

Just like agriculture, you have to change crops periodically or the soil will get exhausted and stop yielding. This is also true of messaging. If you don't change it up, it gets stale and stops growing.

This doesn't mean it's time for buffoonery. Some aspects of changemaking are always a spectacle. However, if the entirety becomes suitable for theatrics (and you're not a performance artist by design), you've gone off-course.

I've seen a certain platitude a lot lately: "Validation is for parking." This sounds very cute and self sufficient in an evolved consciousness type of way, but it's a bit of rubbish when it's not placed in proper context. As social creatures, we all seek validation. It begins with childhood and gets reinforced by society. When we get along with some folks as opposed to others, find our tribes and feel connected, it's because of validation, being seen and celebrated instead of ostracized or dehumanized. It's also a bit of serotonin and oxytocin, but we've already gone over that.

The trick is to find where the validity exists among people of real value to your life and overall well-being. To learn how to, for example, stop hoping for the abusive parent to one day magically give you unconditional love and start to, instead, find fulfillment in the love systems that already exist around you.

Our modern media systems are artifice. And as we keep progressing, finding a brand that has become hugely successful through organic means alone will be like finding a valley of unicorns. Organic growth isn't necessary and in this environment, it's a needless objective.

Find the flow. Find the energy. Find the momentum and ride it or redirect it. It's the same way fashion works. Designers keep reinterpreting what already exists. Every piece of clothing we will know already exists. We just keep playing with how it looks, what it's made of, and who makes it.

26

Always Maintain Direct Contact

You always need a direct mailing list. Never let a third-party channel that you don't own or control be your primary source of direct communication with your community. You must always be able to directly reach your community. Always.

Building a list through other channels is fluid if you create an action plan. Here are 10 ideas on things you can offer or create to build your list for direct outreach.

1. Exclusive Access to ticketed events, downloads, etc.

2. Giveaways + Contests of curated products or services. This can be especially effective when the contest partners with a major brand that appeals to your community.

3. Launching "Community-Created Content" Contests that incentive your audience to create and submit themed content for a chance to win a prize and visibility.

4. Offering Exclusive PreSales of products and services before you release it to the general public.

5. Incentivize Subscriber Referrals by giving discounts or some other compensation for these referrals.

6. Make the List First for Debuts of new products and services so that subscribers receive *insider* information.

7. Segment Lists into particular interests so that you can build even stronger subscriptions for targeted campaigns.

8. Signup Thru Events that are either live in the real world or conducted digitally. This can be a simple reminder to sign up.

9. Signup during Direct Purchases by offering a signup option at the end of the buying event.

10. Free Product Exchange by offering access to your webinars, whitepapers, audio content and more.

YOU DON'T HAVE TO WAIT FOR **A SEAT** AT THE TABLE WHEN YOU BUILD **YOUR OWN TABLE.**

27

Visage. Voice.

Napoleon Bonaparte owned two newspapers. Historians have often noted how brilliant this megalomaniacal icon was at propaganda and getting his face all over the place. There weren't a ton of newspapers back in the 1800's. So owning not one but two says a lot about how he could determine what "news" people received. Yet, to stop at mentioning that alone is a disservice. Napoleon was inspired by Julius Caesar, who lived in admiration of Alexander the Great.

Alexander conquered an extraordinary amount of land between 336 and 323 B.C. His money was respected and worth its weight in silver. The front of the coin showed the face of Hercules. Zeus was seated on the back. These monies didn't just serve as capital. They also peddled culture and the mythical idea of a man becoming a god through Herculean acts of bravery and triumph. Back in Alexander's day, revered imagery was still reserved for the gods.

Caesar had different rules. The statesman is credited for building the foundation of the Roman Empire. He had seized power through a coup and a coup is what killed him. Before he got stabbed to death, he was money. He put his face right on the front of the money. Now, coins didn't just hold the monetary glory of Rome, they also served as an ancient form of viral media for Caesar. This media strategy took the idea of ruler to the next level. Caesar was more than a king. He was his own thing. Caesar became so synonymous with this ultimate status that his name gave birth to the words kaiser and czar.

That's the kind of respect Napoleon truly appreciated. He was a great tactical general but he didn't leave his rise up to just his battlefield talent. He had a plan. Under his reign, the French government spent considerable time and talent swaying favorable public opinion through powerful speeches, bulletins, targeted censorship, Napoleon-authored commentary and proclamations. He also did strategic patronage of the arts in a way that got him associated with and documented by top artists while he also rubbed elbows with societal elites. His image became popular throughout France and much of Europe.

He was noted for saying, "An army marches on its stomach." Keeping soldiers well equipped and well fed was part of his strategy for winning battles, but it also kept favor within the military ranks. The proof was in the results: he won 53 of the 60 battles he fought. His loss was trying to take Russia.

His image-making methodologies crafted him into a timely trope of the relatable heroic revolutionary capable of achieving the military triumphs and subsequent peace the French government seemed incapable of producing. Before crowning himself Emperor, he even commissioned a series of commemorative medals called the *Cinq Batailles* which promoted this very narrative.

If you bombard the system with your image and your voice,

it's almost inevitable that you will maintain a fanbase. But most people think this is a matter of over the top, in your face, heavy hitting 24/7 ubiquity. Culture isn't a firewall to be broken through by a hacker. Not at all. The way to truly bombard isn't through blunt force trauma but through weaving into lots of different things until your image and voice are inseparable from culture itself.

What Napoleon understood about legacy building was a lot. He saw that a cultural shift needed a message, a face and a voice that could maneuver through the intricate system of media. He saw all media as an opportunity for promotion and knew the system was steered by advertising, marketing and public relations.

He tethered his personal narrative to a trope his nation loved and recognized. This, along with his written communication helped build empathy and public favor. He fostered compassion toward himself as a leader by caring for his military. He shaped a message and philosophy that would promote, justify and glorify his coup while also scaling his image to be part of bulletins, medals, articles, art and theater. To think, Napoleon didn't have social media or camera phones. He had to understand scale through old fashioned means, but the equation's elements remain the same throughout time:

Strategy + Scale = Change

28

Scale As Capital Gains

A scary thing happens without scale of a message, mission or movement. Money, time, energy, wellbeing, knowledge, emotions and networks get wasted, misused, and under utilized. This is what makes people feel exhausted and burnt out. This is the law of diminishing returns. This is when the enthusiasm dies and the things that get created lose their spark of inspiration.

The capital you reclaim through scale is your wild, wondrous time to live on this planet. All ecosystems have scale, and your media strategy should be a scaled ecosystem. It is short-term and long-term measures working together over space and time.

Scale begins with an inventory of current assets, an inventory of possible assets, an understanding of what can be diversified, packaged and repackaged in your thought leadership, and an honest assessment of where you need duplication.

Know Your Inventory: this is your entire content bank, your social contacts, your financial capital, your time, and so on.

Create Products: your content bank is going to help you create products. Look for licensing opportunities. Collaborate with others where possible to create cross-promotional products and limited edition goods. Products can sell while you sleep if you set up sales funnels, hire sales help and use SEO to aid the process.

Use SEO: once you know your inventory and what you're rolling out, use legitimate search engine optimization (SEO) and the hundreds of fundamental rules there are to harmonizing with and utilizing the algorithms. This increases traffic, visibility and sales.

Participate in Q&As: go online and find places where your thought leadership can find more like-minded people and offer your insight. This can be answering questions on career forums or actual question-and-answer websites, joining in on social media discussions, or participating in *call and response*. Join panels in the real world. Team up with peers doing tutorials for digital download and participate as an expert. Share and make sure that your sharing links back to other insights, your personal sites and more.

Advertise: use digital ads and adwords to increase reach. Set a budget and be consistent. Even a small investment of $5 can yield results with persistent application and smart targeting.

Publicize: even when you have hired a publicist, you have to be your own. Actively do media outreach. Ask others in your network to keep you in mind while they're doing press. Ask journalists that you speak with directly what they're working on next. Give them referrals to people in your networks. This creates a system of cooperation and cahoots.

Get Duplication: you always need sales duplication. Find help and make sure you include commission to incentivize results. If you need help with SEO, find a part-time expert. Hire graphics designers to aid in promotional materials. The digital landscape helps you find sites with global talent.

Send Valuable Emails: email marketing is still legitimate media, if you don't send spam and vainglorious dribble. What do your subscribers really need? Offer email blasts that are just broadcasting your work. Seek to benefit others. Answer perplexing questions. Curate useful articles from around the web. Provide visibility for others by highlighting their work and making announcements for others.

Network Vertically and Horizontally: connect with peers, influencers, icons and anyone else you can reach who is aligned with your work. Create alliances. Pay people for their time and promotion.

Write Op-Eds: publish your opinion pieces in top-tier to niche newspapers and magazines that hold space for these editorials. The term "op-ed" is short for "opposite the editorial page". These written prose pieces express opinions by an author who isn't affiliated with a publication's editorial board. They're part of the conversational environment around a narrative and many pundits begin their careers by publishing op-eds in outlets across the country.

Collaborate with Brands for Giveaways and Contests: help your community get special, exclusive things by teaming with brands that make sense and doing an exclusive offer for your people.

Gift Them: crowdsource your community for their wishlists on whatever platform you desire. Then, randomly choose a winner and gift them something off their list.

Craft a Focused Portal: if many of your quotes focus around the same topic, consider creating a separate digital portal, like social media, a digital newsletter or a website, just for these types subjects. Quote others who have said great things on your chosen topic. This will aid search engine optimization and, if the people you quote are still alive, allow opportunities for networking. Find services that will help you automate posts so that it doesn't warrant additional time from you. Grow this portal well, and it can also be used to generate advertising dollars from brands and individuals who would like you to share their insight to your portal.

Setup Additional Social Channels: create your own distribution network through multiple social accounts you control as subtopics for your overarching narrative elements. For instance, a musician who also journals song lyrics and doodles can create accounts for each of these aspects — music, journaling, and doodles — and allow the three accounts to share and reshare content through automated posting. They build different audiences that are connected by a shared interest in the artist.

Start Affiliate Programs: focus on a niche product you offer and set up affiliates who will get paid through sales referrals. Locate niche partners who have already built traffic flow with your target audience. Offer compelling content for your affiliate partners to use. Grow the program (or repurpose profits to hire someone who manage the program) and take good care of your partners.

It takes time and strategy to build scale. Choosing an angle of attack and staying consistent with the implementation is the first step toward freeing up your time and using scale for capital gains.

29

Make A Decision, Darling

No one cares what you think. No one cares what you say. No one cares what you do unless it directly affects their life or livelihood. At the end of the day, none of this matters to anyone except for you. Your life is your own. Make a decision, darling. Decide if you are going to listen to your passion.

Self awareness is not a passive reality. The heart, looking inward, reaches out. Self awareness and self compassion demand action. True compassion for oneself compels deeper compassion and love for others. Doubt, fear and disillusionment will creep into your mind daily and every day you will have to do the work of defeating it. People will say things to you and about you that can crush your spirit. You will have to get over your ego. People might do duplicitous things to you hoping to derail your progress. You will need to take countermeasures or plot evasive maneuvers. You'll have to fight for what you believe to be true and yet figure out how to be open to what you may not know or realize. Sometimes, you will fail and you'll have to learn how to balance all those emotions around that failure.

Every day, you will have to bring forth your inner joy. It is a choice. You can luxuriate in the privilege of having a life in which you can choose to answer the deep calling that comes from within.

BE
YOUR OWN
THOUGHT
LEADER

30

The Question and Answer

What do you hope your cultural legacy will be?

List 5 actions you can start taking today to begin making this legacy a reality.

List 3 people upon whom you can rely on for collaboration and successful achievement of your goals.

List 5 people you'd like to receive mentorship from in order to realize your dream. *It doesn't matter if you don't know these possible mentors.*

PART TWO:

BECOME

31

The Primary Objective

Although they don't typically get conveyed as such, branding, marketing, publicity and PR are all part of business development. This is further revealed by the primary objective of PR. It is a deliberate, strategic system of messaging designed to help establish a brand and once that brand is solidified, help maintain that brand as a fiscal entity.

Once this primary objective is understood, it becomes easy to also realize the vehicle through which public relations perfected itself: **it was a strategy of war**.

Repeat this until it resonates. Read it again. Say it aloud.

It aids coups, like it did in the case of Napoleon. It has always been a tool of colonization and imperialism. Long before PR helped corporate brands, CEOs and celebrities, it helped governments and empire makers conquer, rule, discredit opposition, force assimilation, marginalize voices and expand their culture as dominant, normal and desirable. The Hopi have a proverb, "Those who tell the stories rule the world." Public relations is strategic storytelling that determines which mouths tell the stories and which ears listen.

The same techniques that establish an oppressive, conquering culture as gloriously respectable visionaries while representing the conquered and oppressed as savage, barbaric simpletons are akin to ways a PR campaign roots certain images as mainstream and others as subversive, deviant and undesirable. The same barrage of messaging, both overt and subtle, that causes a culture to discard its own value and aspire toward another are the same strategies that help a luxury brand establish desire in the consumer.

Contemplate the strategies of *shock and awe*. This psychological warfare makes the advantaged side believe it is outnumbered, outmaneuvered and overwhelmed. Their belief in their own false disadvantage will in fact cause their actual downfall. This is a wartime use of public relations by relating to the public in a way that alters reality.

Public relations can make the *unreal* a reality. All that's required is belief. In its most benevolent forms, this can be a glorious thing. The same strategy that wages war can be retooled for building peace.

PR is the first storyteller. It directly connects with people, all forms of media, and messaging to implement a narrative idea, seemingly from thin air, and adhere it to our inner worlds. Our belief makes it real and relevant. Our consumerism makes it fiscal.

My suggestion is to not allocate much energy toward feeling things about this. It is and will continue to be for some time. At this point, see the stream and realize there are 3 choices:
1. Get caught up in it.
2. Swim up it.

3. Redirect it.

You can employ a strategy that uses any one or combination of these approaches. To begin, you need to think through some factors about authority, support, originality, opposition, salience, and the value of your time, energy, and effort.

Whenever you're *creating*,
you're *leading*.
You're asserting *your experience*
as an *authority* on
the human experience.

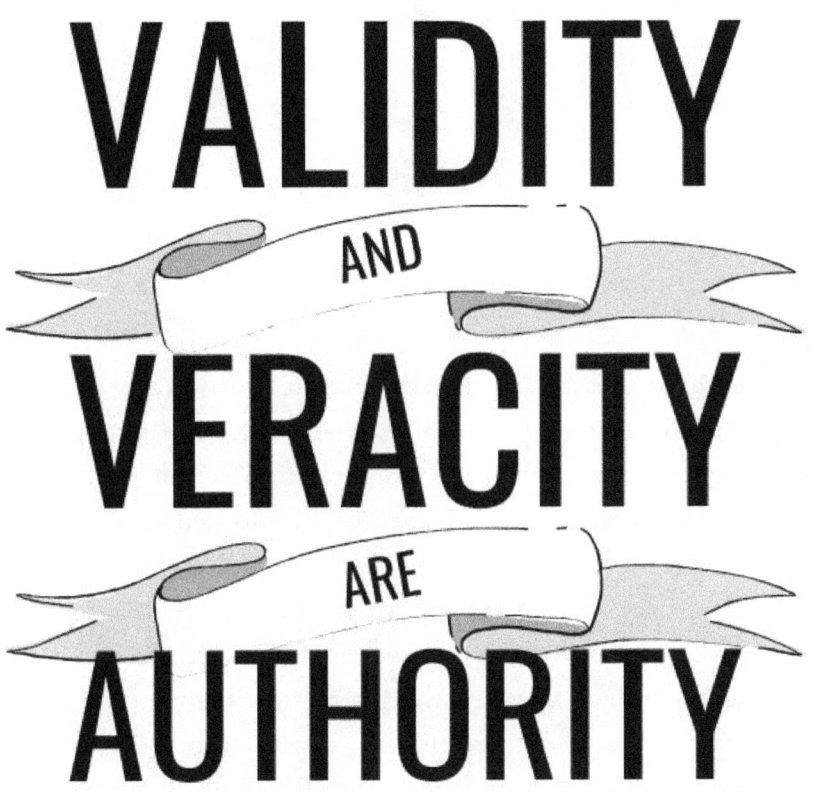

VALIDITY AND VERACITY ARE AUTHORITY

First they *believe* you. Then they *believe in* you.

32

Authority

It's always easier to criticize than it is to create. Creating requires thinking and doing. The creator has to enact the alchemy that shifts self awareness into action, for it's not enough to simply be. The creator feels compelled to also do. In modern life, certain aspects of doing have become synonymous with the terms "influencer" and "thought leader" and "authority." Whenever you're creating, you're leading. You're asserting your unique experience as an authority on the human experience. You're using your perspective to disrupt culture's previous perceptions of the subject matter at hand.

Confidence in what you're crafting gains people's attention, but confidence alone won't encourage sustainable respect. The combination of validity and veracity are authority in most people's minds. Those who present messages that feel logically sound and factually accurate gain admiration. We appreciate that they've done the work of gathering data, analyzing information, fact checking, crowdsourcing knowledge from others, and presenting their findings to us as wisdom. We like them because they're presenting something mystifying to us in a way that peeks past the veil.

First they believe you. Then they believe in you. Their trust bestows authority upon you to keep leading thought.

When our leaders, or those vying for leadership, veer away from sound accuracy, we get suspicious. Public opinion starts questioning all that confidence and wondering if it's just a con. Kowtowing and lying is the work of confidence artists and despicable person. Once the trust you earn starts to feel like it was gained through duplicity, admiration disappears.

Trust is one thing but idolatry is another. I think we should let people be people, flaws and all, so that when leaders mess up, they have a shot at contrition and accountability. Pedestalizing people invites sainthood. Sainthood status requires a lot of editing of a life. We seldom vet our idols. So, as you build authority and trust, don't get caught up in your own hype. Celebration can also be a distraction from your original, pure intentions. If you get thrown off from your center, you'll eventually distort your constructs and accuracy. You'll betray the trust that has been offered to you by your admirers and supporters.

33

A Fanbase. A Support Base.

A *fanbase* and a *support base* aren't always the same thing.

Tropes, when applied to compassionate storytelling, help you separate the passionately convicted from the mildly interested. Compassionate storytelling tests the levels of engagement your community is willing to enact, how much your vision resonates with them and how vested they are in your success.

This storytelling serves as a call to action whenever you are being:

- Shamed
- Blamed
- Threatened
- Accused

Any form of media can be used to evoke compassionate response. Yet, it helps if it's personal and directly from you like an Op-Ed, livestream, interview with a media outlet, or some other form of content that will allot enough time for you to make your statement.

Regardless, the moment needs to be vulnerable. You have to talk about the issue.

In this short doc, you talk deeply about why you do what you do, the love you have for art and for humanity, the hate you receive (and you show actual mail and comments with the names redacted) while you share how that hate makes you feel and why you press on regardless of it.

Being vulnerable, real and raw while also doubling down on your convictions to create art glorifying the marginalized is a triumphant hero standing up to the mob at the gates.

Most of your followers will discover deep compassion for you, if they didn't have it already. Many will receive that short doc and sincerity as a chance to rally around you and become your benevolent community.

Your fanbase will transform into your support base. They will:

- Buy more art.
- Spread the word about you because you're under attack and need to be watched over
- Champion you with kind words and ambassadorship (tell others about you, share your posts/art/messages) so you can keep creating

Compassionate storytelling asks you to be vulnerable, but it also highlights your strength of character and conviction. It galvanizes your supporters in a way that few other forms of media can. It moves the emotional response from observing and understanding, to seeing deeply and being compelled toward action.

Movements begin with empathy and transform into imperatives. Salience might be one of the active ingredients in keeping that flame of compassion lit.

34

Originality Is Overrated

Originality is overrated, at least, in the ways we generally discuss it. Nothing's intellectually new. Everything has been said, at some point, for thousands of years. Whether it was good, bad, ugly, or outrageous, someone, somewhere said some version of it and probably wrote an entire book.

As the personal branding movement has grown, a preponderance of text about the imperative of differentiation has burst forth. This was mostly born from the past 40 years of thought regarding product branding. The belief has been that the only way to get a consumer to buy one brand over another is to *differentiate*.

Therefore, human hours were commissioned in marketing firms to map out a "brand essence" that no consumer would ever see. Presentations were drafted to explain the brand attributes so that the brand could have more personality, and large teams plotted layered paths toward consumer engagement and entertaining content. All these hours have been spent only to discover we might not have been quantifying what really matters.

Research is now revealing that consumers don't actually see one brand as much different from another. Difference doesn't really affect buying decisions or consumption events. Only a small percentage of people within a brand's consumer group really know anything about the brand. Most are buying for some other reason.

We think we do all the ads, messaging, content, word of mouth and creative publicity to possess originality. Yet, the magic probably lies in what we still don't understand about the mind and the human capacity for information. Differentiation might not hold the gravity we've always assumed it does.

The thing everyone and everything is aiming for is mental availability. *Salience* is what helps you be recalled by an otherwise overwhelmed and exhausted mind during a confounding day. Being different might not be as important as being interesting. Within all these battlefields, winning seems to begin with the privilege to *be thought of* in the first place.

Folks don't really need new ideas, per se. People just need to hear old ideas in new ways that create lucid memory. Contrary to current belief, being interesting doesn't even require a lot of effort.

It's not necessary to be the most interesting. The bar is truly set at just being interesting enough for some sort of usefulness within the mind. Be useful enough for a person to think, "What about ____?" or "Oh yea...". Get tethered to an idea of someone's need fulfilment. Once the mind categorizes your offering as a solution or option within a happening, it will grant you real estate within the memory, or salience. This will seem to ring true despite the population of competitors.

The quality of being someone else's eureka moment takes on even more fascination within in-groups. We can be insulted when we get compared to others but we forget that even a contrast is a comparison. Ideologies group people, and people need grouping in order to feel *peopled*. Grouping is also the first step toward achieving peer salience.

Within life's big picture, we actually understand very little. So without comparisons and contrasts, or metaphors and analogies, we would wrap our heads around even less stuff. Throughout all this confusion, we must also constantly deal with a bombardment of people living their own lives, of which we understand very little.

Compared to other species on the planet, we remain children for an extraordinary amount of time. Vast surface area within our brains is devoted to attachment, and the need is so necessary that we can remain attached to even the most abusive of caretakers. Grouping allows us to feel seen and normalized so that we can stop sticking out due to our feelings of otherness and, if anything, stand out due to our true personalities.

Since media is steered and informed by advertising, much research has been done to find out how individuals not only behave when solo, but also how each behaves within a group and therein informs group dynamics. Shared experiences, environments, interests, traumas and difficulties are used as identifiers or markers. From there, pathways are built.

So, the popular kid who feels uplifted, cool, and validated can easily find just as much targeted messaging as the lone wolf who feels beaten down, frustrated and marginalized. There's poetry for feeling interconnected. There are message boards for outsiders. There's music for fighting the power. There are movies for finding your way through adversity.

The more intimately you understand groups and group dynamics, the more you will understand where the wonderment resides within your endeavors. These are the moments that invite salience, that vivid recollection. For you see, the one solid, constant truth of any group is that it seeks something that feels sublime. The reason the group formed was to define the sublime within their own self image.

The wonderment can begin with simply knowing you are not alone in your otherness. Connection and likemindedness helps the anxiety dissipate. Being seen feels like more than just validation. It gets ingested as value and within the group, the individual has finally found a space and place that sees their inherent worth of existence. The mind calms because the group does not see the person's presence in the world as a nuisance requiring a cure. The group doesn't request the person to explain their reason for being because their beingness is welcomed.

Groups help us stop being distracted by our otherness because there are no factions within them making us explain these parts of ourselves. So, we can get busy with the work of sharing, celebrating, collaborating and organizing power. This shift becomes fuel for a sense of wellbeing and is now a different avatar of wonder.

THERE *isn't a* ROADMAP FOR TRAIL-BLAZING.

35

Being Thought of Is Sublime

There are several thinkers who are far more proficient than I on the nuance of salience within consumerism. Yet, no one has been able to fully define the science behind this neuropsychology of this for branding since you're literally trying to outline the alchemy of a-ha. In their 2011 models on brand salience, doctors Julian Vieceli and Robert N. Shaw identify no less than five categories of definition:

Prominence —the prominence and presence of a brand in relation to its competitors in an individual's memory..

Accessibility —the accessibility of memory content relating to the brand.

Associations —the quantity and quality of associations in the mind regarding the brand.

Order —the degree or frequency to which the brand springs to mind during buying or consumption events.

Familiarity — the 'size' of the brand in one's mind and how prominently this allows the brand to spring forward in response to memory cues.

It's easier for a person to achieve all five of these distinctions than it is for a brand. People can affect other people on levels that a brand can't and that "familiarity" is the kind of relationship brand messages longs to acquire with a consumer. It's the type of enthusiasm and energy that runs through a fan base, and even more so, a support base.

There's a story about Olivia Munn, *X-Men* and fan art that feels like cosmic forces aligning. Fan art usually gets discounted as trivial and inconsequential. What a shame. Any form of fan expression, such as fan art, can become part of one's benevolent community and a source of support and lift.

When Simon Kinberg was discussing plot and characters for the blockbuster movie X-Men: Apocalypse, the team sourced Google for guidance. Kinberg told *Cinemablend* that he and director Bryan Singer went through every character which had been a horseman in the X-Men universe, and decided that Psylocke was the most interesting of the characters. He'd recently met with Olivia Munn about the role of Wade Wilson's girlfriend in *Deadpool*, which she had rejected. Munn wanted action. She wanted to fight.

Kinberg recounts, "I said, 'You know, Olivia Munn could be an interesting Psylocke,' so we went on the internet and Googled her images. And one of the first things that popped up was a piece of fan art of Olivia as Psylocke."

This is one of those moments that take years of work to help it materialize. First, Olivia Munn had achieved salience in being thought of by Kinberg in the first place. He and the director then took to the internet, where their hunch about Munn was met with existing fanfare. That type of reassurance feels like synchronicity. It makes everything feel like it's flowing and falling into place.

That's the kind of influence and magic that a fan base transformed into a support base can have on growth.

Network *vertically, horizontally and diagonally*. There are billions of people on this planet. The odds are in your favor to find great allies that harmonize with you. You'll need alliances with peers, corporate brands, admirers/fans, mentors, sponsors, media, high-profile people, rising stars... Most of all, find people who have vision.

Momentum attracts momentum. Move and shake in spaces and places that energize you. With patience and perspicacity, you can find support that challenges you to constantly *learn, unlearn* and *relearn* things about yourself and your environment. You have no choice. Everything about you is supposed to constantly grow.

36

Networks Are Social Capital

A full contacts database and an empty bank account don't match. No one is completely self-made because we don't function in vacuums. Somewhere along your journey, your hustle gets recognized by someone who also has hustle. Your vision inspires someone next to you. A legend or pioneer in your field anoints you as the successor to the throne. You start getting invited into more exclusive rooms. You get referrals to bigger opportunities. Projects get shaped with you in mind and then pitched to you.

This is your moment of lift. It's your benevolent community rallying to support you while you become the hero of your own story. This is the tangible magnificence of the trope and why it's so prevalent in our cultural plotlines.

Identify your comparisons and your contrasts. Your peers are possible allies, collaborators and ambassadors. You can intertwine communities, cross-promote events and help each other establish validity. You'll need to identify your peers, even if you don't know them. You'll especially need to identify anyone with equal or more reach than yourself.

We fantasize about being discovered by our idols, but only 1 percent of the population has that kind of luck. Most of us can begin by being discovered by those standing next to us. Cast a wide net. The process isn't always about finding people with more power to align with and uplevel. It's also about combining your assets and resources with excellent partnerships.

The media system is consistently building and reinforcing pathways around these peers and pioneers. They're creating or redirecting a stream of energy you can utilize.

Allure has its own power and reputation. The more allure you have, the more of a legend you become, like the wizard or the Great Gatsby.

Your peers show you how to:
- target advertising, marketing, publicity and public relations
- find your opposition (you'll need this group, too)
- identify brands, organizations, and other corporate or institutional entities with financial capital who might become your additional allies

You gain and retain peer respect by showing up and doing what you do best. Don't bore yourself. If you're energized, you'll be able to energize others.

37

Our Mentors Are Our Oracles

We often think of mentorship as a one-way street where the mentor shares lessons learned and the mentee absorbs knowledge. In truth, it's a mutually beneficial relationship that exchanges data, information, knowledge and wisdom. The mentor/mentee vibe can also be one of the best catalysts for synchronicity. The sharing of data points, obstacles and projects can inspire someone to divulge info or a contact that they never would have known was useful or needed unless you said something.

It's important to have mentors who are older than you, mentors who are within your generational age range, and mentors who are younger than you. These complex viewpoints will keep your eyes fresh and discourage your sinking into too many bubbles of thought or intellectual ruts.

Mentors can help us avoid a core mentality that makes newcomers feel like outsiders to some inner social clique. They can also help us stay purpose-driven from the purest origins of our motivations so that ego doesn't take over and start calling the shots. They can also remind us to seek commitments from others so that space within the collective effort is reserved for actively engaged supporters.

Core mentality, lack of purpose-driven centering and an abundance of uncommitted "supporters" will show in media efforts. Mistakes start to get made. Self-destructive behavior emerges. People don't show up for interviews. People within the group start fighting for celebrity status with one another. It gets messy and messiness is contagious within business.

If you think that media professionals can't pick up on internal chaos, think again. All that's needed is for one team member to say something on the record and now you're getting the publicity you don't want. Finding mentors who have vision and expand your scope of compassion, perspicacity, and purpose are great allies in navigating or avoiding these pitfalls. They're like a walking, talking crystal ball when you have the right conversations with them.

38

Our Detractors Provide Wisdom

I've never been the "positive vibes only" type. You need a little negativity in your life so you can learn to not take it personally. Don't ignore your detractors. Learn from them. Study them. Get acquainted with their strategy and playbook. Dig into their desires and aspirations. Few people use virtuosity and variation of tactic, so you'll often find that you can understand them quite intensely, very quickly.

Progress is never permanent. It's always under attack by what wishes to replace it or regress it. Spend ten minutes reading Lao Tzu and you'll grasp the importance of knowing yourself as well as your opposition.

The ways in which they respond to you tell you what you need to know about them. Occasionally, they might even make a valid point about something that requires editing, even if their approach isn't constructive criticism.

You can't elevate your mind while your head is in the sand. Your detractors, opponents and naysayers are part of your peer environment. Taking the time to understand their pathology, desires, fears, and pain points helps you see them more clearly. It can even help you find empathy for them in ways that you adjust your messaging and content to better address those who straddle the fence of alignment with you. Making an effort to understand them can make you a better storyteller.

39

Why Some May Oppose You

As you galvanize larger and larger groups of people, there are some elements of cooperation that should be kept in mind. Peer pressure is an obvious factor to consider, but there are other elements that can lead to acceptance or rejection of your messaging, help you predict the type of negative and positive feedback you'll receive and help you understand how to reshape messaging to address or diminish the amount of possible blowback

Betrayal Blindness: coined by psychologist Jennifer Freyd, this is the unawareness, not-knowing, and forgetting exhibited by people towards betrayal. Victims, perpetrators and witnesses may display betrayal blindness in order to preserve relationships, institutions and social systems upon which they depend for survival, livelihood and security.

Tacit Approval: this is silent approval often characterized by not expressing or refraining from contradiction or objection to an action, circumstances or situation. The approval is implied or inferred by the absence of expressed, explicit disapproval. Thus, **tacit consent** is **consent** that's inferred from the silent party remaining silent when he/she had an opportunity to refuse support, condemn or forbid an action.

Institutional Betrayal: this term, also coined by Jennifer Freyd, is structural wrongdoings perpetrated by an institution upon individuals who are dependent on that institution. The types of betrayal include failure to prevent or respond supportively to wrongdoings by individuals (such as sexual assault) committed within the context of the institution. Individuals will sometimes exhibit betrayal blindness in order to maintain the institution upon which they depend.

Cognitive Dissonance: this is a psychology term for the mental discomfort experienced by a person who holds two or more contradictory beliefs, ideas, or values. This discomfort is triggered by a situation in which a person's belief clashes with new evidence that can disrupt the person's previous perceptions surrounding people, places or things.

Unconscious Biases: these are learned stereotypes that are automatic, unintentional, deeply ingrained, universal, and able to influence behavior. While conscious bias is the prejudice that is known, unconscious biases can often be hidden from the individual, as the person often lacks deep inspection about exactly why he/she believes what is currently believed.

There are, of course, even more elements than this to consider, but there are rather large blindspots that get cultivated within people during early childhood. Part of necessary self preservation when a person is powerless to affect change is the ability to lie to oneself. It's part of the brilliant construction of the mind and how it finds ways to help you adapt to your environment, from which you're inextricable.

These roadblocks to messaging aren't necessarily malicious or conscious. Even when they are pointed and cruel, they can have absolutely nothing to actually do with you. You can simply be a convenient target because you're telling an inconvenient truth. In order to circumvent and redirect this type of energy, you need to understand its pathology and how desperately some need to cling to the illusion in order to feel safe, secure, and self determined in the world.

With this in mind, ask yourself these questions whenever you encounter extreme, pointed and impassioned opposition.

How does awareness and understanding of these behavioral tendencies change your messaging strategy?

Will you kowtow and pander?

Will you take time to dispel fears, biased tropes and myths?

Does your empathy towards those you understand the least expand or subtract?

Will you find ways to dive deeper into the layers of your own message so you can be better understood?

Will you accept that there are people who will never receive you or your message for their own personal reasons?

Who will you target?

Who will you ignore?

40

Allure Creates Its Own Myth

The main thing about culture is that it changes. When you don't change with it, you start to feel tired, worn out and irrelevant. I don't think the issue is that people are expected to shift their entire personalities and personas every decade.

I think the way we respond to people who look or sound stuck is much more about our fear-based need for our own evolutionary self-preservation. A lot of us are trying to balance being in this world, of this world, and beyond this world, simultaneously. People who feel stuck in what we deem "the wrong ways" get interpreted as cautionary tales. It's like they've disconnected from culture, in-groups and progress to which they previously so vibrantly belonged or steered.

On the flip side, people who feel too prophetic scare us, too. We seem to be the most open to pioneers. These are the people who know how to read the room and predict the next steps. They're prescient and perspicacious in the exact amounts that are both modern and future-forward while seeming timeless. This quality is such a heady mixture, it almost feels like virtue.

This is what has fascinated me about designer Elsa Peretti. Peretti is a style icon and the creative genius behind some of Tiffany & Co.'s most famous jewelry collections. She's globally respected as master of modern, minimalist design. Her pieces from the 1970s continue to feel modern and current today. Yet, back in the days of disco and the feminist movement, her thinking was very fashion forward. She wanted to design for the empowered women who were reclaiming their sexuality and pursuing their careers.

Peretti designed pieces that felt feminine, elegant, striking and simple enough to work in the boardroom and the nightclub. Her "Bone Cuff" bracelet, Scorpion necklace, Bean pendant, and "Diamonds by the Yard" necklace adorned (and continue to adorn) celebrities, royalty, fashion denizens and stylish women alike.

Out of all her works, and I can happily discuss them all, I want to focus on Peretti's first design — the Bottle necklace. This is a sleek, small and sculptural vase pendant attached to a link chain. Peretti stated, numerous times, that it was inspired by the girls of Portofino in the 1960s who would carry gardenias that quickly wither once detached from the plant. She wanted to make a vase the keep the flower alive and allow it to enhance the neck. Taking cues from vases throughout Italian antiquity, she drafted the now legendary necklace. That's the official story.

But since this 60s-inspired necklace was designed in the 70s by someone who hung out at Studio 54 with Andy Warhol, Bianca Jagger, and Halston, word on the street had a different theory. There's always been a rumor that the vase was for cocaine, not water to feed gardenias. Peretti denied the accusation, numerous times. The more she denied it, the more the piece's allure expanded.

The rumor has never diminished the beauty of the necklace nor its value. An original from the 70s will easily fetch four figures in U.S. currency. Decades later, the designer, the piece's inherent beauty and the necklace's layered story possibilities continue to compound its popularity and intrigue. Tiffany makes new versions of the necklace to this day and while not all consumers know the pieces history or some of the elements adding to its appeal, they know the piece nonetheless.

Allure is a way to welcome surprise and wonder into a narrative. Everything doesn't have to be so cut and dry or black and white. Mystery is a type of gamification that invites outside people to dig for clarity and discovery. Allure isn't deceitful unless you intend it to be so. Ideally, it is fun and playful. It's vital to find the play within the media you create.

41

Say That

Unless you're trying to completely operate in the shadows, you'll have to be public with your public image. The combination of your voice with your image will help you gain a foothold in the media. You've got to be quotable. That means impactful phrases that adhere to your perspective must consistently fall from your lips with pungent, poignant and undeniability.

A deluge of great, quotable sound bites can travel through media with the same popularity and fire of a cat meme. They will introduce your personality and philosophy. Memes are some of the easiest digestible bits of information we can distribute digitally and in the three dimensional world.

Your perspective helps you speak in sound bites. Once you know your specific points of view and talking points that will grow your message, you can start to construct them into quick bits of information. There will always be a challenge to your creativity to find fun ways to convey your message.

Effective sound bites usually contain at least one, if not multiple aspects, of these elements:

1. **Short & Sweet.** Say it in 140 characters or less. That means one or two sentences, max.

2. **Spin Off Vividly.** Take a phrase or concept that's already going viral and add to it or spin off from it. For instance, in a speaking engagement, I took the popular phrase and meme, "The future is female" and mashed it up to state, "The future isn't female unless it's funded." This way, I was able to convey my unwavering viewpoint that progress cannot sustain without money, and movements have to have financial resources. Which leads to my third tip...

3. **Speak Declaratively.** If you're going to give the media your stance, actually say it and make it a solid. Don't spend more time worrying about someone disagreeing with you than you spend making your point. If you're not sure what you're saying, neither is anyone else. If you can't stand behind it as you say it, then just keep your mouth shut.

One of my favorite Coco Chanel quotes is, "In order to be irreplaceable one must always be different." Nothing about this statement minces words. It's like being slapped in the face with wisdom. Plus, it's so on point about human behavior that it will stay relevant for the foreseeable future.

4. **Rinse. Repeat.** Yep, I'm telling you to repeat yourself. It makes your words memorable and humans learn through repetition. In fact, most of us have to receive information seven times from three trusted sources in order to even remember a fact. So we're innately cool with repetition.

You can repeat a key word that will have buzz, an entire phrase, or sandwich your point between a repetitious beginning and end statement. Brooke Shields once drove her point home by saying, "Smoking can kill you, and if you've been killed, you've lost a very important part of your life." The use of "kill" and "killed" paired with "lost" and "life" made the bite very deliberate.

5. Comparison is the Giver of Joy. When humans are faced with new concepts, we understand these foreign ideas better if they can be linked to things we already know. So, if you want to lodge an idea in someone's memory, compare something to something else, even if that comparison is actually showing that there's no comparison. Known knowns, unknown unknowns, known unknowns and unknown knowns can all be compared to themselves and one another. You can do this with metaphors and similes, comparisons/contrasts or through straight analogies.

As storytelling trailblazer Jordan Peele found himself in 2019 with a second box office hit entitled *Us*, critics and reviewers started comparing the African American auteur's genius with white directors who came before him, stating things like, "Jordan Peele is the next Steven Spielberg." This jarred some readers who were acutely aware of the roadblocks so many directors of color have faced within the studio system. For them, the statement felt tone-deaf to how rarely black stories starring black actors have been held with any reverence. So when @WolveyJohnson blasted the comparison with his own contrast, it went viral:

"Jordan Peele is not the next Alfred Hitchcock or Steven Spielberg. He's the first Jordan Peele."

6. Poetic Prose Goes Far. Rhyming, alliteration and assonance are all wordplays that keep sound bites memorable. Think when Johnny Cochran stated, "If the glove doesn't fit, you must acquit."

This technique comes with practice. Waiting until cameras are in your face to learn is too late. One simple way to hone the skill is by learning to construct phrases in 140 characters or less. This is very digestible and distributable. Also, small versions of the message helps you speak it over and over and over again until you make yourself sick. You have to make yourself disgusted. Speak it until you are tired of it so that it's constructed on a solid foundation.

Always make sure that your sound bites have a digital and/or physical destination. Your words and voice need to be part of your strategy for scale and benefit the overall vision by supplying it with word of mouth and money.

Create Memes: Turn your quotes into memes watermarked with your logo or digital destination. Use them for marketing and backlinks to that destination.

Create Products: Apparel, coffee mugs, day planners and more can be easy ways to repackage and repurpose your sound bites for additional passive income.

Commission Art: Work with artists to turn your words into multimedia experiences. These works can be applied to merchandise aspect or used as street art installations if you make those contacts and connections.

Sound bites are strategy. Merge them with products and projects for duplication of your message, marketing, and monetary opportunities. Load your words with power, insight, and punch and they'll stand out from the noise and surface chatter. They'll naturally become more memorable.

Challenge *Yourself.*

42

The Checklist

Journaling is a beautiful process for times of provocative self-exploration. Notate your thoughts and then check-in once a quarter to see if what you're creating, communicating and currently working on align or resonate. Edit and amend your responses where needed. These responses are guidance, not dogma.

1. What is your distinct vocabulary for your core beliefs? What are you naming and claiming? How is your languaging helping to reframe the cultural thought?

2. Can you clarify more?

3. Where does your community put its subconscious? As Julian Ufano-Leon explains, "Your cell phone is a metaphor for your subconscious." We constantly place our subconscious outside of our own bodies. It displays itself in everything from our fashion sense to what image becomes the wallpaper on our

mobile devices.

4. How is your individual experience enhancing or interfering with your media strategy and growth? Are keeping your content personalized and energized?

5. What lies and distractions need to be cleared away so that you can pursue your goals without hindering yourself and your growth? Are you healing any lingering internal issues? What problems keep popping up in your messaging, teambuilding, media outreach or strategy? Is a personal issue the culprit of this repeated interference?

6. What are <u>all</u> the existing societal and narrative tropes that your narrative taps?

7. What are your storytelling talents? In other words, what tools (like public speaking, illustration, dance, style and so on) can you use to communicate your story to the outside world?

8. Are you exploring all media channels that are relevant to your growth, including niche and tertiary outlets with strong, engaged audiences? Are you using these outlets and feedback from their audiences as research and development for new ideas and products?

9. Where's the oxytocin-building opportunities in your method? Can it be used to further energize your community?

10. What capital do you have? What capital do you need? What capital have you gained?

11. What media channels have you been under-utilizing/over-utilizing? How can you expand outreach and talk to more varied audiences? Are you prepared for any detractions you might receive from veering outside of your normal routine and target demographics?

12. Who are your biggest allies and supporters? How have you supported them recently? Is more reciprocity needed?

13. Have you recently asked for help, referrals and mindful opportunities from your inner circle, community or investors? Do you need to?

14. Are you existing beyond the committee or is public opinion and fear informing all of your decisions? If so, is it keeping your content from having even deeper impact? If not, are you getting too ego-driven and maintaining a balance of mindfulness about the lives of others, especially your community?

15. Are you cultivating allure? Has your media become too transparent?

16. If you have recently experienced trauma, are you dwelling in it? Is it influencing your content, interviews and relationships

with the media? Are you attracting trauma? Do you need to bring forth more inner joy? Do you need to take a break and be quiet?

43

Alliance Is the New Hustle

The guru is dead. No longer can one person hold all the knowledge, all the methods, and all the connections. Big cultural shifts are enacted by the collective mind through complex multi-tiered strategy and collaborative effort. It goes beyond networks and networking. This includes strategy and predictions in cultural directions. The right team sees what's gone unnoticed and sees around corners.

Alliance is the new hustle. You don't have to do the exceptional alone. Actually, the exceptional is entirely too difficult to do without some sort of support base. If you really want to succeed, allow your vision to attract other visionaries. Build a team of highly capable, passionate supporters in the form of colleagues, allies, confidants, mentors, co-branding partners and change agents. You can craft this ecosystem even if you're not at the helm of the message.

At the center of this ecosystem is the collective vision, what I refer to as The Wonder. This is the idea that sparks the sublime storytelling process, creates content that builds community and serves as the talking points for all inspirational figureheads,

pundits and advocates. But leadership develops around that core idea and that leadership needs support to turn that cultural shift into a cultural legacy. Three distinct groups of community provide the necessary support for leadership to thrive:
1. **Collaborators**
2. **Confidants**
3. **Companions**

Collaborators help leadership not get too isolated, bitter, vain or exhausted. They serve as creative juice, wake-up calls, and agency. They share workload and get things done. They can be figureheads in their own right stepping in on occasion to amplify media coverage for the vision. They are a leadership's:

Inspirers: these are the wonderment makers. They have a charismatic way with words and reassuring presence of mind that folks gravitate towards. They are the frontrunners, talent and vehicles for awareness and outreach.

Strategists: these are the big picture thinkers who look at systems and find pathways. They often enter as consultants, advisors or freelancers with specialized skills that are vital to growth and development.

Dealmakers: these folks make money flow and momentum pop. They act as agents, sales talent, or business managers who are constantly putting opportunities together so that things never fade or fall off.

Liaisons: these are the people who like to directly and

diplomatically relate with media, the public and community managers. They might be publicists or family spokespeople, personal assistance or administrative leaders.

Organizers: these operational geniuses understand the workflow of projects, budgets and team dynamics. They are often co-founders, COOs and heads of operations, project management or even creative directors.

Benefactors: these investors are in it for the long haul. They believe in the mission and vision and are willing to put up money or other capital to sustain it. These can be heirs and heiresses, cause-based investors and donors, fundraisers and so on.

Stars: these influential entities can amplify messages because they already have media pull. These can be celebrities, politicians, entertainers, socialites, grand dames of society, megastars, icons, and legends. Their star power provides more platform.

Secret Weapons: these are the folks no one saw coming. They have key connections that help drive results and can vouch for the validity of the vision. They help recruit and grow the community. These are often grassroots organizers, campaign managers, sales agents, recruiters and other brilliant networkers.

Confidants nurture the soul of the leadership. They focus on wellbeing and safety, help to remind key people of the fun and mystery in life when things feel too heavy, help everyone stay focused on the vision and service to one's calling for personal fulfillment. They encourage time with family and friends to decompress and replenish. These are the:

Sages: these naturally curious visionaries analyze and articulate the connections between anecdotes and data. They can appear as academics, thought leaders, or activists.

Healers: these inspirational leaders help energy flow and encourage self compassion. They are often spiritual/artistic.

Protectors: these forceful, loyal people are warriors at heart. They see danger and help leadership think through danger zones. They can appear as lawyers, accountants and security advisors.

Companions are the people who help a leader stay grounded in friends and family, live a full life, and have more than the work. These are:

Kin: in the form of blood relatives, extremely close friends who are the family which has been chosen, significant others, children, spouses, and a remembrance of one's ancestors.

Keeper: the familial ties holds the legacy and lineage of the vision. Sometimes, in the event of the leader's death, one of these people serves as a spokesperson and dealmaker to keep capital flowing into the estate and overall cause.

All of these entities impact the overall media strategy. Aside from offering different types of support to leadership needs in general, they also provide different pathology and insights into stakeholders, ambassadors and community members. They have unique data points that can provide insight about adversaries. They also help highlight where emotional reparations are lacking for the affected communities. This information helps you pitch the big vision.

When the Reverend Dr. Martin Luther King, Jr. was feeling discouraged, he would often call renowned gospel megastar Mahalia Jackson just to hear her sing. Jackson was a devoted supporter and campaigned for civil rights alongside King in the most dangerous parts of the segregated U.S. The two shared a strong alliance based on respect, admiration and inspiration. This bond will even influence Dr. King's world-famous speech during the 1963 March on Washington.

King had to quickly make a huge impact on a live audience of 250,000 people. This audience count didn't include the television viewers and those around the world who would later see footage of his speech. King's adviser, Clarence Jones, recalled that the team was debating two leitmotifs: the idea of a bad check written to the oppressed, or the idea of a dream. King began with the bad check and discussed how so many at the march that day "have been the veterans of creative suffering" from police brutality, racial segregation and discrimination in everything from housing to home ownership to voting.

He cautioned against despair and began telling them to go home knowing that somehow things will change, but his words weren't revealing how things might shift. That's when Jones remembers the world-famous gospel singer calling out to the world-famous preacher as if it was Easter Sunday. Jackson mandated, "Tell them about the dream, Martin! Tell them about the dream!" Her voice can actually be heard shouting this on tape from the march. According to Jones, King glanced in Jackson's direction, put his written speech aside, and begins to improvise "I Have a Dream."

It's a shame that most people don't hear the entire speech. Dr. King's collected words don't just tell people what they've been through, but also acknowledges what they're made of and sees what is possible, yet still invisible, for humanity's future. In other words, he takes the listener to church. This historic moment is one example of why your team matters. We have to surround ourselves with visionaries who are capable and passionate so that when opportunity arises, it can be recognized and seized. We need collaborative thought and collaborative action. Our lives require orenda.

Orenda is a Huron word that refers to the spiritual force inherent in all people and environments to affect the world or effect changes in their own lives. It's a conscious and collective energy of animate and inanimate natural objects. The storm and wave possesses orenda. A song, a bird, a shaman can all put forth orenda. Orenda allows you to change things at will. Orenda even gives you the confidence to trust others' help in expanding your actualization.

You may not amass a team of all the different kinds of collaborators, confidants and companions, but just like with Dunbar's number, you need your core of 5 and your group of 12-20 key people with which you share trust and loyalty. Loyalty is trust. Trust is currency. Many people will go about things alone because they feel isolated, violated, jaded and overexposed. If you can build trust-based networks, you build an advantage. Network until you find the support you need and deserve.

Thinking **is a** *collaborative* **process.**

Thinking **without** also *dreaming* limits the legacy.

44

Mentors Can Be Sponsors, Too

Over half a century before Yayoi Kusama became the most famous living artist in the world, she was feeling stuck and stagnated in her native Japan. The then 26 year old artist didn't feel like she could catch a break. She was desperately seeking signs and clues about what to do next, when, one day she stumbled upon the work of a pioneering American artist... Georgia O'Keeffe. Kusama had attended an exhibition in Japan, saw O'Keeffe's work, and became enchanted.

O'Keeffe and her verve was exactly who and what Kusama had been needing in her life. There was just one little hiccup. Kusama had no idea how to contact this famous artist. It was 1955 and there weren't personal websites let alone social media.

She also knew that they didn't know each other at all, so this would be a completely unsolicited attempt to make contact. Nevertheless, she was able to get O'Keeffe's mailing address from the exhibition organizers. Kusama sent a hopeful letter and some of her own artwork to O'Keeffe's residence in New Mexico. The letter began:

November 15, 1955

Dear Miss O'Keeffe,

Will you please forgive me to interrupt you while you are very busy, and let me introduce myself to you? I am a Japanese female painter and have been working on painting for thirteen years since thirteen years old. As a painter who feels to live very closely with your in respect of the attitude toward art or should I say who feels keen interests in your work, I have been looking for the way to make friends with you for long times.

Kusama went on to state in the letter that she wanted to have a full career as an artist. O'Keeffe actually responded, and although she advised it would be tough to make a living in the states as an artist, she advised Yayoi to come to the U.S. O'Keeffe even made some gallery introductions on Kusama's behalf in hopes of getting her placed. In an interview published in the Guardian on May 21, 2016, Kusama was asked, "What book changed your life?" She responded:

"When I was young, a stroke of luck led me to a book with paintings by Georgia O'Keeffe. I dreamed of going to America and escaping my family, even though I knew no one there... I wrote to her. She responded with great kindness and generosity. Her letter gave me the courage I needed to leave for New York."

Georgia O'Keeffe's mentorship changed everything. Yet, O'Keeffe didn't coddle her or hold her hand. She responded, encouraged Kusama, and vouched for her. Kusama did the rest. She was brave enough to identify her mentor, reach out, introduce herself and accept what her very busy mentor could offer in terms of time and guidance. This is mentorship in the form of sponsorship.

Yayoi Kusama and Georgia O'Keeffe would only meet one time in person. Yet, the kindness O'Keeffe extended was the mentorship Kusama needed to flip her own script.

ALLIANCE IS THE NEW HUSTLE

You Don't Have To Do The Exceptional Alone

45

Spread Out

True strategy can't exist without scale. Depending on how your search the term "scalability", this wide idea can mean everything from the ability to navigate profit and demand to how to increase your time and financial capital. Since we're focusing on cultural legacy and using media for ideological transmission, let's dive into the aspects of scale that relate to reach and opportunity for financial stability.

Content without distribution is silence. Content is King, but... Distribution is Queen. Nothing's going to happen without the ideas and imagery associated with your endeavor finding people. Distribution is needed for salience to occur. Distribution is the mechanism that helps that engaging content find audiences and make an emotional impression that will later turn into a recall when it matters most. Without distribution helping you find and connect with people, your chances of being thought of for any opportunity, financial or otherwise, decrease.

This is the moment that you get to play with all the possibilities of media: **Earned. Paid. Owned. Shared.**

Earned media is any word-of-mouth attention or publicity

achieved from promotional efforts other than advertising. It's essentially free media mention. Both public relations pitching of feature articles in magazines as well as search engine optimization that improves your organic search ranking are considered earned media. You didn't pay for it and you don't own it, so it has been earned.

Paid media is when you pay-to-play on a third-party media channel you don't own. This all forms of advertising and brand integration, since a monetary exchange created and solidified the terms of the media placement.

Owned media are the channels you directly create and control. Your website, direct mailings, and other distribution avenues that you can access as needed. The content you can create for your owned channels include employee stories, user/consumer/audience stories, podcasts, and masterclasses.

Shared media are all your social platforms. These aren't listed under owned because while you can directly access them, you don't own them. You have a user agreement and your account can be frozen at any time. These channels do, however, offer opportunities for brand and charitable collaborations, co-branding with other allies, and engagement with supporters as well as detractors.

Now, here's the big secret. None of these media options by themselves are an effective strategy. Simultaneously engage all three tactics. Not choosing all three will lead to lopsided expenditures of your time capital and it will cripple your potential growth. Your owned media still needs the additional distribution that earned and paid media provide. Paid media needs owned, shared and earned media so that your message gains more validity. Without owned media, your earned and shared media won't direct audiences back to channels that you control, so you won't have the opportunity to expand your mailing list and retain the audience reach you gain from the earned mentions. Earned media coupled with paid placements through shared media can help you gain velocity within your target audiences because you start to create more reference points for your existence. It makes it easier to remember you exist.

Some media systems operate like breaking news. These postings must behave like an event, with urgency, and it spreads as such. The lifespan can be up to 3 years if it's interesting or evergreen enough to keep being shared.

Other systems without an urgent news cycle have longer lifespans. With news, everything has to be hot and immediate. In other systems, the word or visual can keep spreading, being discovered, collected, added to and reblogged or reshared. These lifespans increase to 5, 7, sometimes even 10 years since discovery never goes out of style. So it might not have the immediate sexy eyeball impact as the news feed system, but it has a much longer life and can actually generate more attention in the long run.

I make this point to show that it's a combination of short game and long game that wins. The system has to draw conclusions and then build flow around those conditions. The algorithm helps by ignoring noise to get to the quickest response possible. Noise and nuance is your advantage.

Within the media's system design, popularity is just a representative for where money and money-making opportunities are concentrated. The more the system identifies money hotspots, the more money flows to that area in marketing, branding, influencers and celebs. The areas of possible prosperity attract people just as gold brought pioneering miners to California during the 1800s. People flock to the places where things happen. Your targeted media has to have an air about it where things are happening. This way, the questions of, "So what? Who cares?" become irrelevant because they exist beyond them.

People often make the mistake of thinking system bombardment is the key to success. You can't just take any boring, limp idea and knock a whole through the noise as if you're hackers breaking through a firewall. It has to be fundamentally interesting and from there you craft targeting media to help it find people.

Disruption that gains legs also finds the flow of opportunity. Motivation, capability and opportunity have real-time effects on possible success with targeted media, just as these factors play into team dynamics and collaborations.

The right paid, owned, shared and earned media can tap narrative, craft new stories, disrupt old tropes, and unlock mystery. It can help you respond to mysterious issues in ways that turn detractors into loyal advocates. As long as people have passion, there's workable energy to engage a new conversation or demystify an old, convoluted one. Where there's mystery, there's always opportunity.

The moment that you get stuck or don't see results with your targeted media outreach, stop and reassess what you think you're seeing. Nothing moves without energy. To tap into people's time and ability to align with your messaging and help it grow, you must give them energy that incentives them in return. Ask yourself:

What will motivate people to engage with this media?

Where do they feel capable of finding alignment, growth or success in relation to this motivation?

What factors will help them sense opportunity to share, advocate, or connect?

These answers can then be implemented into your paid, earned, owned and shared media for you to try engaging again. Constantly asking these questions and diving deeper feeds your campaigning with fresh energy.

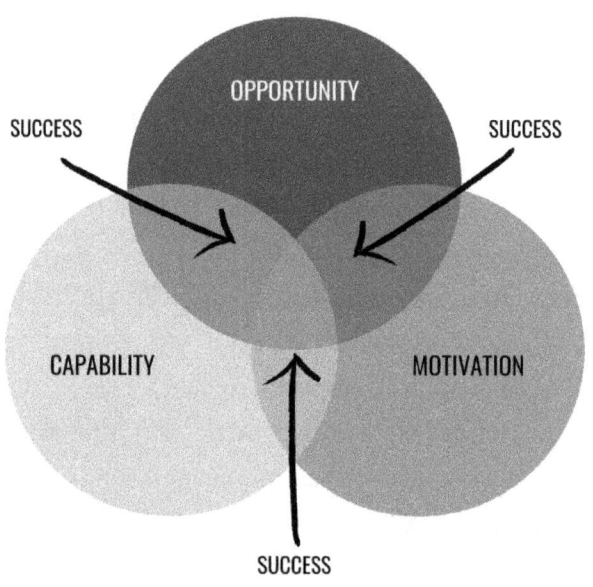

Where there's *mystery*, there's always *opportunity*.

46

You Better Tell 'Em

Repetition is part of how we win narratives. Consistent redundancy is its own form of persuasion. An idea that exists in varied, repetitive abundance eventually stops being called into question as long as it's existence isn't disrupting a person's daily life too much. It's disarming, but repeating something isn't the only way to relax someone's guard. There's also *"presuasion."* Don't bother searching for this word because it's not proper English. I call it presuasion because it's a kind of persuasion where "to be forewarned is to be disarmed."

If you've ever had a loved one get in a car accident, the easiest way to calm down is to know immediately that they're alive and that nobody died. This *presuasive* knowledge makes everything else more manageable, from the car getting totaled to dealing with the insurance company. A little forewarning conditions our senses.

Cults use conditioning for compliance and conformity. They shock the system of a member to measure their reaction, ability to handle abuse and "move to the next level" as has been stated by Dr. Janja Lalich, Ph.D., a sociologist, cult specialist, author, researcher, and retired professor who has spent years studying high-control groups. The measurement of one's ability to handle abuse is what Iceberg Slim, an American pimp and influential author, called, "knowing the mileage on a ho." This is strategic cruelty being implemented to distort a person's inner narrative, sense of self and sense of reality. It helps determine a person's breaking point and therein their usefulness to the secret agenda of control and dominance.

I share this because I want to convey how deeply influential these methods are. Planting seeds in someone else's mind should never be handled with insouciance. Even if your intentions are benevolent, so many can and have used the same insights for abuse.

The implementation of presuasion is a balance of allure and timed transparency. Information held close to the chest gets released in pieces to stoke curiosity and speculation. The pieces of the story that are shared help normalize the idea to people and create pathways in the mind in order to allow for a route of least resistance.

Imagine you're famous, wealthy, well connected and could run for president. You already know other people would like you to run because of surface chatter, blogs and well publicized pleas from other famous names. You can start planting the idea by first denying you have any interest in running. People then start begging you to reconsider. This public outcry becomes its own narrative, therein inspiring vlogs, articles and opinion pieces about what would be great or awful about you becoming president. You eventually announce you're considering running if you can gain enough support. Now, support starts calling you and volunteering to help. You eventually announce you're running. It was an entire process, a narrative that built itself into a well-crafted frenzy.

This tango of intrigue and forthcoming details works exceedingly well with the aims of propagation. People become the caretakers and administrators of the idea. They treat the idea as their own, because it seems to have been born from the ether and lacks a bonafide human source.

The timing of what is released how, when and where doesn't always have a formula. Instinct and applied knowledge will guide those aspects as long as the main goal remains preservation; because this isn't only about promotion. First and foremost, it's about protection, remember?

47

Shut Up, Darling

An opinion and a perspective aren't the same thing. A perspective has insider information about the terrain of the conversation. Anyone can have an opinion. Only those with skin in the game have true perspective, even if that insight comes from a bird's eye view.

Why am I making this point? The rise of social media has made it socially acceptable to mouth off about anything. In the spirit of being transparent, raw, unrehearsed and off the cuff, social media stars are rising for being wide open. Unlike movie stars who have management and PR teams vested in their success, social media pundits and content creators are often operating without a net.

High profile opinions can become target practice. If you don't have a perspective, please, shut up. Say things like, "No comment." or "I need more information." Also, and I can't stress this enough, don't make content about things you know you don't understand and haven't prepared (in any way whatsoever) to tackle.. Research, find experts to guide you, or sit down and do nothing.

On the last day of 2017, Logan Paul, a Youtube star with over 15 million followers, thought he had powerful insight about suicide that he should share with the internet. He was wrong. Everything would have been better if he'd just done nothing.

When Logan Paul and some of his friends visited Aokigahara, a forest on the northwestern side of Mount Fuji in Japan, they entered the woods with video rolling. The thick forest is infamous as a national and international destination to commit suicide and is often referred to as the "suicide forest". So, not surprisingly, they encountered a dead man hanging from a tree.

It's reasonable to assess that the entire group was in shock as they beared witness. It's logical to assume that they didn't know how to process seeing a man who had become so distraught in life that he'd chosen to hang himself. The Verge reported that Paul cracked jokes, laughed and suppressed laughter, again most likely attributed to shock. The group zoomed in on the dead man's body and documented each other's reactions. According to The Verge: "The group continue to stand around the body, filming one another's reactions. Paul is seen struggling to suppress a laugh, saying "this was all going to be a joke, why did it become so real?"

The footage didn't end there. The Verge: "Back in the parking lot he films the emergency response crews, drinks sake, and says: 'That's the life, this daily vlog life. Guys, I said this in one of my first vlogs, I have chosen to entertain you guys every single day.'"

All of this footage, the group's awkward reactions, and clumsy documentations would have remained private if Paul hadn't posted the video to social media. He entitled it, "We found a dead body in the Japanese Suicide Forest…" The public reacted was furious. It a PR pile of stinking hot mess.

What Paul had miscalculated was a lot. Although he stated that he didn't create or post the vlog for the likes, and the post wasn't monetized with ads, many speculated that his decision was still attention-seeking. In his subsequent written apology, he professes, "Let's start with this - I'm sorry. This is a first for me. I've never faced criticism like this before, because I've never made a mistake like this before." He spends most of the apology talking about himself and his emotions as he admits that "it's easy to get caught up in the moment without fully weighing the possible ramifications" because of the sheer amount of content he creates "EVERY SINGLE DAY."

He claims he was hoping to evoke a "positive ripple on the internet" and increase suicide awareness, possibly even save a life. Some applauded him for being accountable. Others found his lengthy, self-focused apology coupled with his actions even more disingenuous. So, he then had to apologize again in another vlog and apologize several times in public.

Paul started off wrong by not entering the woods or the subject matter with a true perspective. It seems he just had opinions and those are insufficient tools when grappling with complex topics. He had no previous history of being a thought leader about suicide prevention or how to deal with losing a loved one to suicide. He's not a journalist, so he didn't know journalistic codes of conduct when encountering and reporting a suicide. Paul entered the forest with a group of people as ill-equipped to handle it as he himself was. There wasn't a professional amongst them well-versed in suicide, depression or emotional health.

For me, Logan Paul will forever be an example of the value in shutting up and sitting down. When facing rough, multifaceted topics and scenarios for which you are under-prepared, just shut up. When you mess up royally, make a short, sincere apology that focuses on how you never plan to do that mess again and, then, shut up. The closed mouth catches no feet.

48

Don't Feed the Frenzy

There's never a news cycle feeding frenzy to be had from the headline "So and So Had Nothing to Say About the Thing". Stick your foot in your mouth though. Sound like an uninformed idiot, and that can go for weeks, be turned into GIFs and become notorious.

You may remember when I explained how PR was perfected as a war tool. The battle isn't always about publicity and advancement. At least 50 percent of it is about protection. There's so much power in opting out of a conversation. There's even more power in using the silent moment to listen.

Every statement shouldn't warrant a response from you. This is especially true if it's mostly rumor or cruelty disguised as a talking point. Moments that can only get oxygen from scandal require your comments to keep it burning bright.

49

How To Release but Lay Low

A journalist once asked me for the best PR advice I had for anyone in the public eye. Although I was never a crisis manager and many have far more knowledge in the practices, I focused on a strategy that falls within that category and always served me well.

Wait until after 5:00 p.m. on Friday to release news you want to fly under the radar. Everyone has left the office to enjoy the weekend and most media outlets only have a skeleton crew working. For the most part, social media won't pick up anything until it's been reported by a major outlet. It may get chatter on social media over the weekend but by Monday, the urgency has fizzled. Usually, the fresh week will offer a new pertinent or scintillating breaking news item.

Still be smart. If you're in entertainment, don't pick an awards weekend to drop the Friday news. Everyone on the red carpet will be asked about your story and it will be part of the Monday morning cycle.

50

Cycles

Our news is a 24-hour cycle. Timing is no longer the only factor to consider. You must also determine the best angle of attack.

For mass media, big news breaks on Tuesday and Thursday mornings. In the U.S., that means things roll out around 6 a.m. EST so that it's at a fever pitch by the time it reaches the Pacific coast, which is three hours behind. These timeframe also meshes well with the surface chatter and distribution interplay of digital and social media.

The power of digital channels to complement a breaking story is incredible. Microblogging, news aggregation, discussion, and real-time photo-sharing platforms serve the news well as it's happening due to the small amount of characters required for a message/post and the use of hashtags to follow the story as it progresses. Social sites that function more like personal web pages or information discovery allow news to have much longer life cycles.

Where a rapid fire story can fizzle within 2 days on a microblogging network, elements of can keep gaining chatter for up to 5 years on a personal web page social site and up to 7 years on a platform geared toward information discovery and sharing. A current example of a microblogging platform is Twitter. A news aggregator is Reddit. Facebook is a personal web page network is Facebook and Pinterest is an information discovery site. However, the names of the platforms don't matter. Understanding the social network's design, function, usefulness, and methodology are the ingredients to discerning how that channel merges with the news cycle.

51

Repackage. Repurpose. Redistribute.

We forget about time capital but, spoiler alert, we only get but so many hours to be alive. So, there's talent in knowing how to spend it. When it comes to promotional content, the content that furthers the agenda, I have a strong 80/20 rule. Ideally, no more than 20% of your time will be spent creating the content and at least 80% of your time will be utilized to promote the content.

That means that if you have 100 minutes to promote yourself, don't use more than 20 minutes creating the content and use at least 80 of those minutes promoting your content. This is how you have time to create and distribute. Content without distribution is silence.

This is why one of my favorite things to do is repackage, repurpose and redistribute content. There's no need to reinvent the wheel when you can change the rims and slap some polish on the tires. Rock it until the wheels fall off.

Most creative entrepreneurial types already possess a large content bank. Yes, content can be capital, too. You can always draw from this wealth of content from:
- Notes + Journaling
- Blog Posts
- Interviews
- Masterclasses/Seminars
- Presentations
- Speeches
- Email Blasts + Newsletters
- White Papers
- Books
- Social Media Posts

Any of the elements I just listed can be pulled apart and isolated, combined, curated, redesigned and rephrased to become something new. This is the creative process of repackaging and repurposing old content into fresh items that can be redistributed on different platforms.

You can even update an old, nearly forgotten item, and redistribute it to the exact same audience. You'll get a new crop of engagement from those realizing the contents' existence for the first time or from those already acquainted with it getting to see it differently with new eyes.

Repurposing is also a way to continue emphasizing your core passion and core beliefs to an ever-expanding community. No one in your community is going to know all your content unless they are truly obsessed. Someone who newly discovers your community on Friday will most likely have no idea what you distributed the month before.

Take old content and breath new life into it. For example, you can take a tweet, screenshot it, post it to Instagram, then later have an illustrator do an artful display of your same quote to post on coffee mugs or a t shirt. One piece of content used 3 different ways without any stress. This saves time, energy and effort.

Let's play with something I stated earlier: You're human. You deserve to become more than a brand. I have actually tweeted this statement several times. To give it a new consumable form, I decided to screenshot it, and turn it into a meme, and post it to more image heavy social media sites. I've also illustrated it using playful, tropical clipart and bold display text. It then got shared and reposted on even more social sites.

This simple change gave the thought new life and new audience of engagement. These examples are only the beginning. This quote can also inspire the title of an article on my website or be the cover of a journal. One of the illustrations can become part of an illustrated desk calendar of quotes or and turn into a t shirt.

Repurposing your content isn't just about creating more content for more marketing. The gems in your creative bank can be reimagined as products that can be sold or licensed to other vendors.

Repackaging and recycling your content allows you to change the presentation but keep the essence. It can enhance your creativity. It even gets you excited about your content when the feelings have waned and all your messaging is feeling like drudgery.

I also use the 80/20 rule for sponsored content. Just as magazines and newspapers need to have a large newshole, which

 **Joy Donnell Society**
@doitinpublic

You're human. You deserve to become more than a brand.

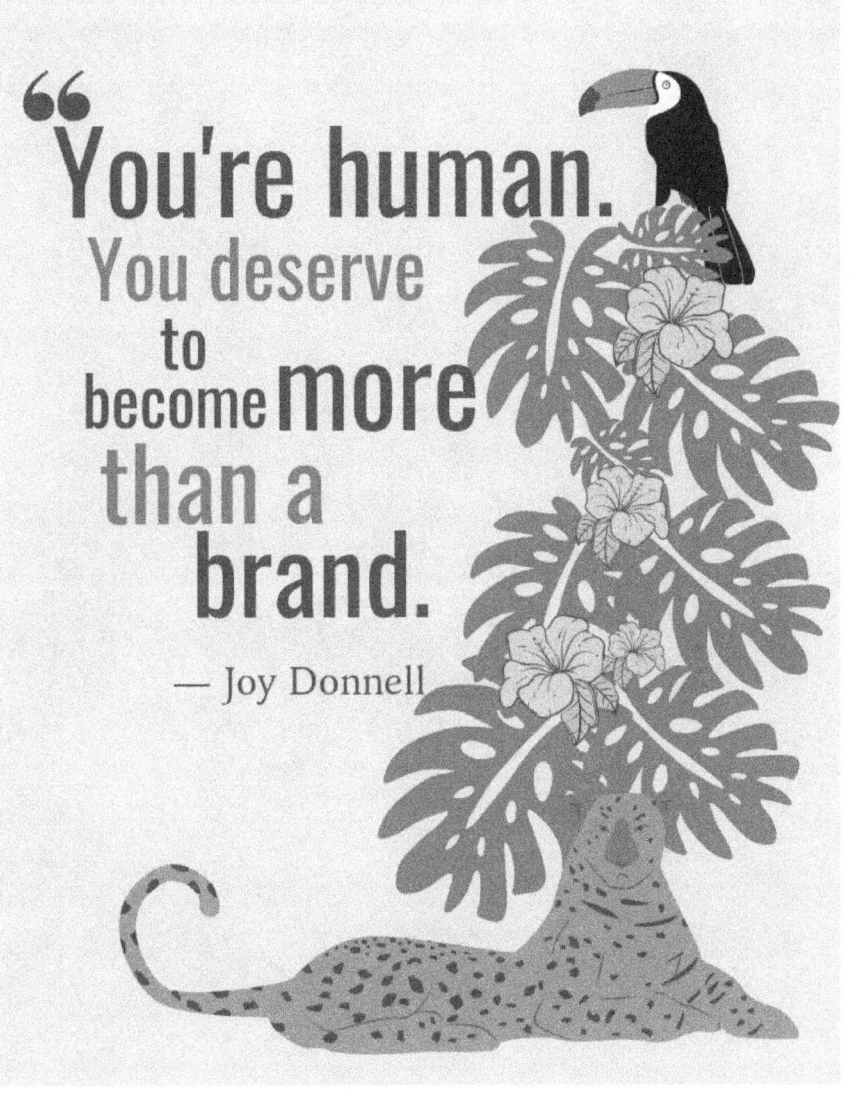

means the amount of news should also outnumber the amount of advertising within each issue, your sponsored content should always be displayed in a smaller amount than your unsponsored content. Otherwise, you have little credibility because all of your content is bought and paid for.

Automation is a secret weapon. Finding the proper tools to aid content creation and distribution is pure freedom. They will increase your time capital and the hours you save not having to do so much direct distributing gives you more opportunities to create and increase all your other wealth.

So, if you publish on your own blog, you can set up an automatic posting of the article's URL to all of your connected social media platforms upon publication. You can then use a repeat content distribution app or service to repost that message and link as many times as you designate at times you can also control. You'll just need to have the service linked to your social media account. While this is happening, you can also have the URL posting to other curation sites that list blog posts through RSS feed.

You get the idea. The process is to find automation tools that share, reshare and disseminate your content for you. Repost, recycle and redistribute whenever, wherever and as much as you can.

52

Loot Your Content Bank

EXERCISE #3
APPRECIATE YOUR ASSETS.

You can turn the bulk of your content into assets and passive income. The key is to package it that way. Explore your content bank and find 10 pieces of content that you can repurpose and redistribute. It doesn't matter how old the content is as long as it's still relevant to you, your message and your vision.

1. See how many different ways you can repurpose each item of content you have in your arsenal.
2. Consider if some of the items can be packaged together into a small series of content.
3. Determine what is possible product and what is purely marketing. If some pieces can serve as both, even better.
4. Find automation tools that will help your content be redistributed further.

Consider This: Recognize that sometimes, *you* are the content you need. Since April 19, 2000, Oprah Winfrey has posed on the cover of her *O Magazine* each month. She often explains that this isn't an act of "vanity", but an effort to make life run smoothly. After booking thousands of celebrities for *The Oprah Winfrey Show*, the iconic talk show host knows how tasking it is to secure talent on a regular basis. It was easier to use herself as the cover model and never go through the trials and tribulations of booking and scheduling other talent. She was the best solution for her own content.

53

Coups, Religions, and Drug Dealers

If you really want to understand how a message gains life force and cultural prominence within media, how a whisper campaign energizes fiscal solvency, and how *nothing* becomes *something*, study coups, religions and drug dealers. When the word "coup" gets tossed around, some of us still immediately think about Caesar and the betrayal of Brutus. But Hitler seized power through a coup. As did Napoleon before him. As did Lenin. And it's one thing to successfully execute a coup. It's another thing to maintain that power once it's seized. The deeper skill is to not end up dead.

It's no wonder that one of the oldest jokes about organized worship is: *Cult + Time = Religion.* Just like cults, religions often begin with a charismatic leader at the nucleus and spread out from there. The difference is that cults seek to manipulate, and religion simply seeks to be a guide during turbulent times like societal upheaval, political uncertainty and catastrophic loss. Religions build something from nothing. With this statement, I'm not criticizing the religion. My point is that it's an industry based on immaterial belief, with rarely anything truly concrete and tangible to present. It feeds the soul. It taps into what people think, feel, fear and hope simultaneously, much like the forthcoming dictator of the coup. Religions present answers to the chaos of life, just as the strongman does. Believe. Trust. Give. Support and everything will be fine from here.

Drug dealers are some of the most amazing entrepreneurs on the planet. Unlike Apple with big billboards on Times Square, drug dealers operate in the shadows, yet they move billions of dollars in product. They are whispers that create dollars. You have a product. You sell the product. You make a profit margin. You reinvest it into the street hustle. That's the methodology of flipping. Eventually, you grow enough capital to diversify the business, and in the most ideal situation, go legit into legal business ventures where you can eventually phase out the illegal activity.

The commonalities of all these seemingly unrelated phenomena are duplication, scale and location. Because there's only so much human capital available from a single person, every venture needs duplication. Duplication can be found in supporters, such as the militia, statesmen, and government allies that back a coup. It can be missionaries for a religion, who go out and bring new faces to the congregation and help find those to covert. It can be sales agents that help a drug enterprise expand operations. Thinking small is how these forces grow big, as they always scale up from a local level. They thereby hold reverence for space and place, giving great thought and strategy to where they go, when they go there and who it is that represents their values and agendas in different environments.

Within media, this duplication, scale and locational strategy looks like ambassadors to spread your reputation, influencers who support and vouch for you, sales reps who help you move product, publicity, marketing, management, and so on. A media strategy is more than content and is wider than conventional thoughts around distribution.

Again, location matters. People who carry the message have to occupy spaces and places where the narrative can find an audience and grow community. It's too much for you to do alone. Build your team. Build your support and let them know exactly what kind of help or guidance you need.

54

Publicity Lessons from Despicable People

Everyone has someone they personally see entirely too much in the media. It's that polarizing person that some folks love, some folks hate and some love to hate. They have a lot of visibility and a ton of reach so they seem to literally be everywhere: always on the news, always in the timeline and always being talked about by strangers at the next table. Somehow, you know where they've been, what they're doing and how much they do it but you don't even care for this person or their version of life. You actually find them to be a bit despicable.

Well, despicable people become influential all the time. How it happens is packed with publicity lessons.

Confidence, darling. Confidence. Often, we wait for level of certainty to occur in our lives before we feel powerful and confident to act. Confidence isn't a requisite of action. Plenty of people have learned how to wear certainty and ego as camouflage. They might be thirstier than a dying man in the Sahara but you'll never know.

Confidence is potent. We admire and crave assuredness. We even kowtow to it. Certainty is such a comforting rarity in our eyes that we'll even substitute arrogance for it.

The Lesson: When people don't feel they get to actualize their own power, there's always the possibility that they'll seek a *chosen one* who actualizes their own. This allows people to see themselves reflected in this individual's image and message. They gain a vicarious strength and within that, they experience the sublime.

The news tires quickly of insecure people. Insecurity is tragic and gawked at for a while only to be abandoned for being too predictable. Tragic is always tragic. Certainty can do anything. Anyone using confidence as a strategic skill knows that news cycles will give the same attention to tackiness as it does grace so long as it comes with certainty.

Stand Up. Some controversial figures assert that they are only being considered *controversial* because they're unapologetically giving voice to the voiceless. They're not going to take it anymore and they will, often single-handedly, correct the injustice.

The Lesson: There's always a group of people feeling underappreciated and vilified. The controversial figure offers themselves to the media as a spokesperson for this group.

They Treat Celebration, Toleration, and Disdain the Same. An individual can only expand their influence but so much by strictly preaching to the converted. Messages need distribution. You already know that distribution evangelism exists within the groups that celebrate you and automatically love your message.

A lot of positive people avoid negativity. Those polarizing people welcome it and use it as momentum, just as they ride the energy of favorable response. As long as people are talking, yelling, arguing and verbally vomiting, there's some energy to work with and spin. They'll even purposefully do something that gets everyone riled up just to create distraction and tabloid style news. As long as they make you look, they feel like they're winning.

The Lesson: A little emotion goes a long way. There's visibility among those that tolerate your message, even if they don't engage. Yet sometimes the most media energy comes from disdain.

Controversy is a Strategy. Which headline will get more news cycle: "Superstar Says Earth Round. Sky Blue," or, "Superstar Says Earth Flat. Blue Sky is Computer Simulation"?

It's a tricky tactic. One thing the instigator relies on is that their core audience will ignore the confusion. The most loyal fan's own cognitive dissonance won't allow him/her to give the controversy too much oxygen. So ultimately the noise will be made amongst the group that despises their message, which is just more publicity for their cause.

The Lesson: This isn't a strategy that can or should be applied constantly, but a carefully timed boost of controversy that creates confusion always causes chatter. When people ask questions, they're striving to understand. Striving to understand is a path toward empathy. Of course, it can also lead to people concluding that the individual is certifiable and therefore irrelevant.

The Real Perception is Perception. Social media has flooded our lives with all the voices. Every identity group feels different about everything and for the controversial outlier, this presents a wealth of opportunity. When you craft the narrative from all sides, the story gets obscured.

The Lesson: The only real perception is perception. Two-sided narratives share the same base storyline that's usually rooted in a common fear or human need. This is why it's easy to have two very different opinions floating around the same issue.

The narratives can take up all the oxygen and obscure the emotional heart of the issue. Slogans work for energizing in-groups because these pithy phrases encapsulate entire emotional cues around a narrative. Stepping into a narrative, or shaping and reframing a storyline, without first understanding its root emotion is dangerous and lacking real strategy.

Speaking It Aloud Normalizes It. We're vexed by those who co-opt disruptive language. We're shocked when someone twists, distorts and reconfigures language for their own agenda and gains. This vocabulary shift changes the game. Now, words that used to help us guide conversations in particular ways have become vague constructs with multiple connotative meanings for different identity groups.

The despicable person uses this disruptive language to legitimize themselves on a public stage, divert shame as well as accountability, use media to craft their own mythologies and court media for publicity's sake.

The Lesson: Language is a living, fluid thing. Narrative battles begin and end with vocabulary. You can't remove the mind from the body, the individual from the environment, or the culture from the context. When we lose context, we lose languaging.

Keep Finding Ways To Talk About Yourself. If speaking it normalizes it, then that includes controversial people being able to normalize themselves simply by continuously talking about themselves. For their fanbase, this is pure oxygen and they want more. This only annoys people who are already annoyed, and, again, their disdain is more energy.

The Lesson: Popularity is momentum. It has an energy of its own. Although it should never be a solo goal — because it doesn't offer wellbeing, only a false sense of validation — it can still be utilized for media reach. It's a part of how salience grows.

The public figures who annoy us the most still have loyalists who support them and keep them going. What are the ones we admire doing to garner our respect and energy?

55

Publicity Lessons from Admirable People

Everyone has someone they personally can't see enough in the media. It's that cool person that some folks love, some folks hate, and some love to hate. They have a lot of visibility and a ton of reach, so they seem to literally be everywhere: always in the news, always in the timeline, and always being talked about strangers at the next table. You know where they've been, the wonderful things they do, and what they're working on next. You actually find them to be a bit admirable.

Just like despicable people, admirable folks become influential all the time. How it happens is packed with publicity lessons.

They Believe. Belief is infectious. It's the food of conviction. People who share their views in emotionally connected ways speak to us on deep, psychic levels. They tap what wish for in our own lives. It can be about life, systems, our beliefs, justice, ownership, or things that seldom get discussed.

The Lesson: While we like to treat logic as being separate from emotion, the two are interwoven. Our logical responses are still informed by emotion, even if we're basing the logic on ignoring the emotion. Thinking, after all, is a collaborative process. So strong belief relates to our logical emotion and holds space with our individual aspirations.

Speak Out. They stand up, speak out and speak for what is right. It resonates. They give voice to the voiceless. They express what we're all thinking with common sense and urgency.

The Lesson: There's always a group of people feeling unseen, unheard, and marginalized. The admirable public figure consistently uses their platform to amplify the issues and needs of these groups.

They Don't Give a F*ck. They may bend but they don't break. They don't care about push back and bullies aren't going to stop them. They know how to ride the waves of celebrators and naysayers. They double down on conviction when faced with severe opposition.
The Lesson: Don't get caught up in the drama. Also, don't get caught in the trap of exhausting your energy explaining your very existence on the planet. Positivity and negativity are both fickle. Their usefulness is the energy they provide the storyline and

spark deeper conversation around the talking points.

Conviction Is a Strategy. Which headline will get a longer news cycle: "Superstar Says Nothing About Anything," or, "Superstar Says They're Not Backing Down"?

The Lesson: When you're living a life of solid reputation, standing your ground is viewed as a noble act. Perhaps it's even a modern form of *noblesse oblige* and expected from those who have garnered access and name recognition. If their conviction is met with more bullying from the opposition, their support base rallies around them with opinion pieces, surface chatter and rhetoric to drown out the undesirable narrative.

Stay Flexible. Great leaders have to listen while maintaining dialogue. When their viewpoint adjusts over time, they acknowledge the faults in their former opinions and welcome a different lens on the subject at hand.

The Lesson: Growth warrants respect. Past beliefs that held back progress don't have to be ignored or buried. They can be acknowledged as data points to illustrate how much you have leveled up in thought and wisdom.

Saying It Aloud Brings Attention to It. They expand, redefine, and rearrange language for a broader viewpoint and agenda. They reframe narratives to be more inclusive and a call to action for course correction.

The Lesson: Look, listen and find the white space within the media coverage. Where the breaks in understanding exist, there's also mystery and opportunity. This is the space where new vocabulary can be introduced and new narratives can be birthed.

They Dig Deeper. We already know some things to be constants. We can now go beyond data collection and use the info to expose deeper knowledge. This feels like voluntary evolution. It keeps the conversation going because these admirable thought leaders are constantly sharing deeper insight and strategy toward a fuller human experience.

The Lesson: Evolution is a natural way to keep conversation flowing. Spotlight seeking isn't necessary because the work has its own energy and popular presence. The more knowledge is shared, the more salience the work acquires in the minds of others.

By now, you've probably noticed that these actions of, and lessons from, despicable people and admirable people mirror one another. That's because who we respect and who we loath is often based on the context of their tactics and quality of their reputations in our individual eyes. Context is a determinate. Context is a beholder.

If you were dying of thirst, would you rather be handed a glass of water from Mother Teresa or Hitler? Some people would say Hitler because they like him more. Some people would say Hitler because their culture celebrates him as a great leader. Some people will say Mother Teresa, because they admire her more.

And some will say Mother Teresa because they dislike her less than Hitler. That's the environment in which we play.

56

The Shame Blame Game

Opposing viewpoints can actually be held upright by the natural tension they create between one another. When this happens, the media system frames both "truths" as valid content streams. Anyone who is inclined to manipulate the story completely can use these dual truths to flood the media with noise and misinformation.

How does this happen? You start with the two narratives shared base storyline. This is typically founded on something that is commonly feared, loathed, or craved. The easiest American tropes that correspond to these categories are elitism, fame, wealth, and being special and/or chosen. There are groups that fear, loath or crave any of these identifiers at any given moment. For instance, there are conspiracy theories that think liberals are lizard people just like there are other conspiracy theories that purport conservatives are lizard people.

The next step is to take that base storyline and nuance it with one noticeable yet imperceptible thing that puts it on the next level of the story. This can be something like conservatives being warlocks versus liberals being witches. Pitting the evil masculine against the evil feminine is a next level move.

From there, the two stories keep branching off into competing yet complementary narrative plots that will continue to balance each other by pushing equal tension against each other. Shame and blame are the fulcrum that maintains the balance. Think of how conservatives fear socialism and liberals fear authoritarianism. The connector is that both sides fear being ruled in a dystopian manner but this common concern gets obscured by the rhetoric of shame and blame.

A culture's collective health and collaborative levels can often be determined by how quickly it uses shame and blame as an alternative to accountability. Where the culture lacks inclusivity and/or institutional and individual onus, shame and blame will be employed as a last ditch effort towards restorative justice <u>or</u> maintaining the inequitable power structures. Even though the language of shame and blame can distort the core emotions within the narrative, they should also be a signal to probe deeper

Disrupted groups can feel empowered once they identify either a scapegoat or a villain, but this categorization only magnifies a shadow. The real culprit is the *thought virus* itself and the ways this infection keeps groups from fully discussing and disclosing their true values through more production dialogue.

Media muddles the conversation because, as a system, it has no collective obligation to clarify anything. Both narratives have energy and financial resources poured into them to keep them vibrant and viable. Remember this as you craft narratives within the media.

The only party responsible for the story is the storytellers.

Ask questions of the tropes with which you over-identify as well as those with which you under-identify. Examine how these ideas are pitted against one another. This information will help you better understand what the real motivations, fears, disgusts, and needs are at the heart of all this communication.

Find the real data and knowledge before you map out your plan. Talk to people who have better perspective. Don't get caught up in the drama of the other storylines. Infuse your messaging with the actual emotional content and specificity.

The specificity is the universality because it cuts through the surface chatter and dives into the core values, beliefs, dreams and humanity of the stakeholders. This is what speaks to people and provides uplifting energy because it goes beyond the tired, overused enthusiasm-sucking dribble. Saying it aloud brings attention to it. Once you have the emotional truth coupled with the understanding of the systemic facade, you have messaging that redirects the stream. Find the media forums that make sense, and everything will build.

This is why you must always look deeper. It's vital to question the origins of the stories we tell ourselves about ourselves. Especially as we tell stories to others.

57

But Who's Winning the Narrative?

We get laser-focused on being right. Everyone thinks they're the one who's right. We argue about it. We defend it until our last breath. Yet, in the logic of media, it doesn't matter if you're wrong or right if you're not winning the narrative.

Advocacy is about impacting public opinion. Impact is about relevancy. Neither of these will happen without first understanding what people believe, why they believe it and how attached they are to those beliefs.

Our tropes around the constructs of power and celebrity often make us think that we need big, popular voices to shift narratives in our favor. This isn't true. Fame that doesn't resonate can actually be a minus. There's a saying about how a simple lie travels faster than a complicated truth. Being right doesn't play well in the media unless it has an impact.

Resonance > Fame.

It pains me to admit this, but for many of us, Impact is Veracity. Change begins with finding the actual narrative and filtering out all the noise. Not all information is good information and the noise will misdirect your progress.

You must eliminate:

1. **Paid Content.** Before you push this content to the side, make sure you understand their consistent message, such as slogan and other short, central thoughts that get conveyed in the advertising.

2. **Shallow Noise.** Idle chatter, whether praise or complaints, that don't share any real insight on impact or sentiment.

You'll need to stay knowledgeable of your topic signatures. These are the most popular sub-narratives within the overall narrative. There are usually at least 5 topic signatures that connect to favor, impact, and emotionality. They should include the narratives that are in alignment with as well as opposition of the overarching narrative.

Now, return to your checklist. In light of this new information, have any of your thoughts changed?

58

Narrative Defense and Offense

Narratives are always on a battlefield, whether we're aware or not. Every rational viewpoint is considered irrational or dangerous by another. We will never all agree. When I see 100 people agreeing on everything all of the same time, I always assume someone is lying.

The belief and reality around something will never shift without building both a defense and an offense. This is how you care for the cultural shift. With that in mind, there are 6 keys to positioning a narrative:

1. **Identify All the Narratives.** You'll need to understand all sides of the story and what is driving thought.

2. **Rank News, Data and Insight.** Filter out the noise and rank the news, data and other analytical information you

gather by relevance. Not all media outlets are equal. Where is favorability? Where is disdain? Where is momentum? Where is engagement? Do certain types of outlets resonate better for narrative engagement?

3. **Determine All Drivers.** What fuels the narrative? Is it tethered to old tropes? If so, which ones? Is it being shaped by current pressures?

4. **Find the Opportunity Zone.** Building new narratives take time, energy and effort that you probably don't want to expend. Take a closer look at the noise. The noise contains data, too. Sometimes it just helps us understand emotional variables related to the narrative. Sometimes the noise helps us find the opportunity to redirect the narrative.

5. **Craft the Strategy and Action Plan.** Once you've mapped all the narratives, ranked the data, identified the drivers, and figured out the narrative opportunity, you can construct your strategy and action plan. Leave room for malleable reconfigurations.

6. **Measure Narratives Over Time.** How does/has the narrative changed or shifted? When does it trend? When do different Topic Signatures experience upticks in awareness or urgency? What are those upticks tethered to?

Your strategy, action plan and measurements over time will require some additional steps. First, you want to tether the narrative to any key tropes that already have funding and vested interest within the system. This can be found in everything from existing advertising, to mainstream op/eds, to complementary narratives om tertiary media channels, to adword campaigns. You can specifically use paid content to piggyback your narrative onto these tropes.

On Disruptive Narratives: Avoid all narratives that disturb the sentiment building you wish to achieve and steer clear of discourse that will shift conversational focus when you're not trying to expend resources on oppositional ideas.

On Undesirable Narratives: Redirect erroneous narratives by unraveling their logical constructs with solid examples of facts and sources. Reframe the narrative to a storyline that honors a broader vision and continues to explain why the previous treatment was lacking in scope or relevance.

On Marketing Narratives: Amplify the narrative through ambassadors, influencers and all other resources that can relay the message with sincerity and accuracy. Where possible, gather influencers who once embraced the undesirable narrative but have now changed their viewpoint. Hire them to be ambassadors.

Never underestimate how many people use cruelty as a strategy. When designing narrative action plans, if pays off to be mindful of how many opposing constructs will emerge simply to bombard the zeitgeist with bad information to undermine the possibility of clear understanding. Having strong defense and offense plans will help you employ timely countermeasures as the need arises.

Opposition will always exist. It's a distraction. While you'll never be fully beyond it, you can constantly do the inner work and outer work that helps you be prepared for it and reframe it. Just stay focused on building your wealth alongside your vision. This is part of protecting your energy and that's bigger than any singular distraction.

Alliances grow narratives. Align with experts who have insight where you are ignorant and perspective where you only possess opinion. Build teams and give those team members room to flourish in within their element. Help them claim their wins. The goal is to develop people, not diminish them.

The Secret To Success:
DO WHAT YOU DO BEST AND DELEGATE THE REST.

PART THREE:

BEYOND

59

Now

You cannot separate your mind from your body, your personhood from your environment, or your culture from its context. They've all been informed by one another. As you build, and experience more growth, you'll need to constantly examine yourself, your surroundings, the cultures you encounter and all of that context. You are forever a student.

If you've chosen to work toward a vision that is bigger than yourself, then you've also chosen an infinite process. Your inner work begins with voicing your intention, mapping your core passion and listing your core beliefs. This, in turn, expands your definitions of <u>you</u>. Your ideas of wealth get wider and taller. New vocabulary emerges.

Your outer work understands the media system and how it requires content, distribution, and advertising of narrative streams. With new eyes, you look at your own assets differently.

You better recognize how to use what you've already got, as well as what you're continually creating, to monetize, market, and build. You know you need a team and support, not just fans. You speak more fluidly to your community and the overall stakeholders. You outline how to use your core passion and beliefs to create deeper messaging, enact a strategic but mutable. living plan that uses a combination of paid, earned and owned media to keep finding audience, allies and lift. You recognize narrative struggles and the pitting of dual storylines. You stay with the emotional connectivity, keep infusing your content and method with energy and oxytocin, and harness conviction.

What now?

Whatever you believe is what you'll build. Persistent, concentrated effort will always yield results. Your results will most likely manifest a certain level of the success you seek in order to feel like your life is moving with purpose. This success is where the real work begins.

All that struggle, planning, implementing, redirecting and resiliency that was necessary before the success was simply the beginning. It was the caterpillar preparing to cocoon. And while it's one thing to successfully cocoon, it's another thing to have the power to burst free of the cocoon.

Success changes your surroundings and the dimensions in which you play. It shifts what you plan, how you plan and who helps you plan. Different pressures apply due to team, responsibilities and expectations. Some advisors will encourage you to coast and maintain while others will advise dramatic leaps and swerves. New levels of confusion will arise.

You'll be challenged to decide:
- What battles to fight...
- When to diversify, wait, or let go...
- How to keep building wealth that supports your growth...
- Who to entrust, avoid, fire, and seek out...
- Where to cultivate synchronicity...
- Why to even bother...

No one will be able to decide any of this for you. This is where strategy and surrender converge. But if you relentlessly pursue self-awareness, remember to be kind to yourself, and implement whatever backups you can for your risk-taking, you'll improve your chances at figuring it out. Afterall, no one is prescient. We're all guessing along the way. It's just that some of us are making educated guesses.

60

A Luxury Mindset

I always felt weird about the way luxury was portrayed in the media. The imagery always expresses over the top decadence and opulence. Lately, it displays *expensive* as its own fashion statement. Our media suggests that luxury is the presence of excess, but true luxury is the absence of angst.

The items promoted through luxury marketing are seldom necessities. This is an industry highly skilled at creating desire from thin air; studying its theories can help anyone better understand the language of want versus need. Luxury isn't found in things; its discovered within moments of emotional calm. So if the things you acquire only bring you more financial or emotional angst, then it's not real luxury.

Those who think of luxury as what is exclusive and rare might find this outlook strange. Consider this: inner calm is the real rarity of this world. So few of us have adequate time for deep self-evaluation and awareness. This is the luxury of self. If you forge your strategy from a mindset of lack, not just around your resources but also from within your own self, then lack is what you will build. You build what you believe. Your media strategy will be anemic.

An abundant notion doesn't invite the end of pragmatism. It welcomes more savvy. It's a different type of hustle.

Through consulting, I've discovered that most people already have what they need to start rising. They know someone that they forgot they know. They were handed a business card of someone key to their growth, but they never followed up. They stopped letting their contacts know about what they were working on or striving towards. They have a unique gift, talent or skill that they never considered redirecting to gain momentum in a different area.

These simple disconnects result in huge momentum gaps, encourage sedentary frustration, and waste time. No one would own a warehouse business and neglect to keep track of inventory. Yet, we do this to ourselves all the time and our strategies suffer for it.

It's a bold realization to recognize yourself as the abundance in your own life. The bounty you seek is already within you and of you. This outlook changes the way you deal with rejection, pitching, synchronicity, ego, fame, opposition, outreach, negotiations, and message building. Mindfulness is a state of being and a state of doing. Emotional intelligence and mastery doesn't just protect you during this journey, it centers you while chaos flings everything around you to the four corners.

This luxury mindset in particular helps you appreciate the ways that intention also requires preparation, skills development, and concentrated effort. See what you've already brought to the table and then bring more. Sometimes, recognizing abundance in your life is realizing you've already done the work, you're already overqualified, you've been ready, it's already yours, and right here, right now, is your time.

61

How the Process Feels

We all contain a lot of noise. Rarely is a person static and truly predictable in terms of mood and response. We can ask someone a question at 11am and then ask the same question at 5pm and get two completely different answers. Most of us are easily capable of duality.

So, as you move forward, know this:
- You will get bored.
- You will get anxious.
- You will get challenged.
- You will get tired.
- You will get celebrated.
- You will get appreciated.
- You will get tolerated.
- You will get vilified.
- You will get ignored.
- You will get embraced.

All of these things are distractions. They all function as signals for you to make choices, adjust strategy, check in on your emotional well-being, or rise to an internal call to action. Again, mindful approaches are a way to ease your understanding of what you encounter.

Search out the level of play within this. Put puzzle pieces together and move yourself around. You'll either grow your fun or your despair. Please, pay attention.

62

Own Your Power

Behold this life that you have and all the power that comes with simply taking up space in the world through your body. Space and place dances with our power. Our environments and social behaviors can help us become closer to or further from ourselves. How your image and your voice appears in the media landscape is an extension of your life energy. Populations of people are using digital media to preserve their public image. For many, there's no longer fear that one will leave the world without there being any trace of their remains.

Using your energy to publicly promote your image is one kind of liberty. Using it to bring attention to a cause or necessary cultural shift is another form of might. Directing your energy into protection of your own image and the images of others is a completely different type of channeling.

Hazel Scott was the type of performer who didn't just

demand dignity for yourself. She utilized the power her public image had afforded her to maintain the dignity of her coworkers.

She was a musical prodigy. The Trinidad-born jazz and classical pianist, actor and singer entered the world in 1920 and was attending Juilliard by age 8. By age 16, she was performing on the radio. In the 1930s and 40s she became a headline attraction at both the downtown and uptown branches of Cafe Society. During the days of relentless racial segregation throughout Amerrica, Scott became known for Jazzing up the Classics, in which she took classical masterpieces and jazzed them up with modern sound and virtuosity.

A captivating performer, Hollywood wanted to get in on the Hazel Scott business, too. The film industry, however, didn't offer many options for a pioneer like Scott. Black women were usually portrayed as maids, cannibalistic savages or a complete joke. Their bodies were used to juxtapose and create comic relief or fear response.

Ms. Scott ventured into Hollywood despite the lack of representation. Leaving nothing to chance about how she'd be presented on screen, she exerted her human rights through her legal agreements. Her contract always dictated forfeiture if her audience was segregated. Her acting contract stated she reserved final approval on script and wardrobe. Her credit on any film would always be, "Hazel Scott as Herself." This type of control is pretty much unheard of today by any race or gender, let alone back then. These firm rules guaranteed that there would be zero onscreen maid's uniforms in Ms. Scott's acting future.

Her contract (and resolve) was tested during the filming of "The Heat's On," a 1943 patriotic musical. In a scene where nine black soldiers are being bid farewell by their sweethearts, Scott plays the piano and sings upstage. The dignified men are going to war for their country. For some reason, wardrobe thought their black female loved ones would be decked out in dirty aprons.

Ms. Scott was disgusted. She told the choreographer that she wanted the wardrobe protections of her contract extended to the extras on set. It didn't matter if she was presented elegantly. The piano prodigy knew that no self-respecting woman of that day, who was also in love, would possibly see her man go off to war wearing a dirty apron.

Nothing got resolved on set, so Scott went on strike for three days. Her standoff was costing the studio too much money, so it acquiesced. The final scene shows the women in clean, vibrant floral dresses as they send their men off to war.

This big screen victory temporarily paused her Hollywood trajectory. She said, "[My brashness has]... gotten me into a lot of trouble. But at the same time, speaking out has sustained me and given meaning to my life." Since she wasn't getting offered movies, she toured, quite successfully. Scott was making $75,000 annually, according to *Life* Magazine, and this made her one of the top-earning musicians of any color at that time.

There was too much financial possibility for Hollywood to continue its silent feud with the virtuoso. In 1950, Scott aired *The Hazel Scott Show*, making her the first black person to have a TV show. The variety show featured Scott as its solo host, and a black woman had never gotten that type of billing on the small screen in U.S.

Things were golden, until societal fears attempted to tarnish everything. She got accused of being a Communist by the House Un-American Activities Committee, or HUAC. The suspicious frenzy that permeated the Cold War was too much. Scott's show got cancelled. She went to Paris where, as she told Ebony magazine, she was able to take "a much needed rest, not from work, but from racial tension."

While her American fame dimmed, she continued playing across Europe, North Africa and the Middle East to adoring fans. Much like the philosopher Voltaire, Hazel Scott wasn't dependent upon one economy alone. Her career and her public image was global, which meant her opportunities could extend beyond her own country and its systemic fears. Talent such as hers can't stay buried. Her legacy and the cultural legacy she furthered grows stronger everyday.

A new generation is discovering Hazel Scott's courage and grit through rare recordings and film scenes of her dizzying piano playing and vocal prowess now posted on social media. Her legacy is being given new life because she always stood for something and used her talent to honor the dignity of others.

Hazel Scott is an interesting example of using contractual clauses to protect one's public image and cultural legacy, using talent to build a wide career, and being so financially viable that your demands for dignity must be maintained.

Yet, sometimes the constant gardening is required after death. Our images can outlive our physical bodies. Thought should be applied to how you show up in the world once you're gone. This is especially true if you hope your image will continue to affect positive change.

Look at the Jimi Hendrix estate and the icon's image in a violent action thriller episodic for Netflix. "Altered Carbon" is sci-fi noir detective novel filled with aspiring immortals, murder mystery, corruption and a reluctant hero in Takeshi Kovacs. In the book, one of Kovacs most meaningful allies in the Hendrix hotel, an AI hotel with the central theme of, you guessed it, rock legend Jimi Hendrix. Like any responsible executive producer and showrunner, Laeta Kalogridis approached the Hendrix estate for the production rights to use the icon's name and image. The estate turned her down.

"The Hendrix estate doesn't license his image for anything that they consider to be violent," Kalogridis tells *Variety*. "And our show definitely, as does the book, has some violence."

Hendrix was not public domain, but other options are. Eventually, the writers' room decided to substitute gothic writer Edgar Allen Poe, which supplied an even creepier air to ways the AI bonded to Kovacs. Regardless, the estate was able to ensure that Hendrix's message (and image) of love remains intact beyond his physical life. Without an estate to continue protecting his image and honoring his voice, how else would this edict have been sustained?

I've personally witnessed the heartbreaking effects of a leader dying without a will, an estate or a foundation. It's an undue burden placed upon the heirs. It causes chaos and it often keeps the legacy from truly thriving because parameters weren't put in place. Part of your power is in exacting how you relate to and empower the living, even after your death. If you are working toward legacy, never think that death is the end of how you will show up in the world. Help your trustees be guided in ways that still honor your purest intentions.

Self care is the **most underrated leadership skill**. The key to resiliency is *self compassion*.

63

Are You Having Fun, Darling?

After a while, people get sick of hearing the same thing and folks get tired of saying the same stuff. In the south, we call this being "farted out." It's just a less boring way of saying how dusty and busted, overplayed and overexposed something is. Dealing with the media for a long time can at first be very excited, but eventually feel routine and exhausting. Next thing you know, you stop having fun.

There are usually two types of boredom. There's the knowledge of being bored but trying to power through. Then there's the boredom that creeps up on you. Both are opportunities for joy.

When you're bored and you know it, that's a good sign. It means you're paying attention. You don't have to accept this condition on a personal level, let alone with your media content. You're bored because you're creating within your comfort zone, but not your element.

We get busy and overwhelmed as endeavors grow. That's

when we start negotiating with ourselves and rationalizing turnkey muscle memory. We don't think. We just ride the comfort zone hoping to sustain actions that aren't sustainable.

Our element is the environment in which we're naturally suited to be dynamic and thrive. Contrary to popular belief, this isn't always a relaxed state. Spaces that are accommodating for your virtuosity are sometimes bizarre and bewildering, inviting you to be vulnerable about confusion. They might be mundane and require more of your innate wit and humor. They might be frustrating and demand you come up with creative workarounds. The cure for boredom is imagination.

Other times, you're stuck in a rut because you haven't given yourself enough time to get bored. Building is a slow, diligent journey. It takes up cognitive space and time capital. It requires investment of your human energy. There's always something to do.

If you fill all your time with tasks and people — leaving only enough spare moments to bathe, sleep, eat and use the bathroom — then your best ideas are getting buried in your mental noise. Boredom needs to take you by surprise. A forced break can be a great disruption. Getting quiet and calming down the adrenaline allows new, sometimes daring, ideas to burst forth.

With enough creativity, you can document the mundane in ways that are hilarious and relatable. There are videos online right now about people unsuccessfully assembling Swedish furniture that with make you snort with laughter. You can also share confusions and confoundment in ways that help others realize that they're not alone. You track your journey toward deeper knowledge and invite others to share their stories. You can get so frustrated that you start devising cooler ways to share graphics, data, and stories that impress you with how visually fun they are. There's always an app to help make content be more vibrant.

Whatever you're fired up about deserves your joy to balance the aspects that are rough and saddening. Media is one area where you can have fun, even when the messaging usually requires a serious tone. Breathe joy into your passion by being dynamic, as much as possible, with your content.

64

You're Creative Whether You Like It Or Not

Here's the thing: your creativity is going to come out in one way or another. If you don't nurture and allow it to develop within your work/art, your hobbies or your growth, then your creative mind will get channeled into the ways you worry and the anxieties that overtake you. It will merge with how you develop disappointing, drama-fueled relationships, and the convoluted thought-mazes you construct to rationalize and justify the fiction you tell yourself about yourself. You'll even use it to normalize other people's messiness so that you can survive it or avoid dealing with it directly.

Instead of using your talented mind to build towards something you really want for yourself, you'll use all that imagination to reinforce fears that hold you back. Because you're here to create. It doesn't matter if you believe you're creative. You're going to create something each and every day... one way, or another.

Perhaps you'd prefer to put that energy towards creating cultural legacy, fundamental wellbeing, and your full human experience. Consider this: Maybe you're the magic you seek in your life.

65

Stay In Your Energy

GROWTH IS A PROCESS OF GOING:
Inward. Outward.
Onward. Upward.

Think about a seed rooting into the soil. The power to burst forth and sprout is concentrated within its center and, from there, that seed erupts and changes its environment forever. At first that change is a disruption until it finds harmony with its surroundings. Like seeds, the life force that will fuel your vision, resiliency, joy, and content is your own. Words and visuals are potent, that's why you're seeking to use them to further this thing you want to further. That's why you're harnessing the power of media.

For sentient beings, reaching out and growing into the environment comes with some inner responsibilities to other sentient beings. We are all stewards of a cause and an effect. If we live long enough, each of us will at some point do something that has an effect (good or bad) on someone else. And vice versa. That is the influence of being alive. While we can't be expected to be accountable for every unforeseeable outcome of the content we create, we can at least be mindful about where we're coming from when we begin to create.

Remember, this is about sublime wonder. Magic is a heightened awareness of what is invisible, yet possible. To stay in touch with that energy and infuse it into your content, you must be courageous enough to keep going inward before your reach outward. You must keep going inward so you can keep moving onward. You can reach inward to keep pulling yourself upward.

Grow. Don't coast. Don't get complacent. Stay excited. If you're bored with interviews and your own self-produced content, sit down. Reflect. Find your energy. If you're anxious and frustrated, sit down. Find your peace. If you look through your content and you're not inspired by yourself, sit down. Find what's going to blow your own mind.

Even if your energy is introverted rather than extroverted, it's still palpable when you're lit up from the inside. We serve each other as energy, like batteries or spark plugs or refueling stations. If you've run empty, you're going to put out empty. Fumes will only offer more fumes. If that wasn't enough, fumes will also attract fumes.

Be mindful of your content. Messages are magnetic. What you put out will come back to you. So, if you lose your intentions and pure motivations, you'll get messy and that mess will permeate what you create. If you get bogged down in the cycles of routines and obligations, you'll lose your joy and it will permeate what you create. Self realization is the realization of your focus and reason for doing any of this in the first place.

You will constantly need to get quiet and reflect, forgive yourself and let go. This isn't a stagnant process. It never ends, regardless of what kind of life you choose for yourself. It will help you be clear about what you convey. That clarity will resonate outside of you and energize others. The vision will gain fluidity and harmonize with more people. So keep reading culture, building resources and investing in yourself. Inward is your seed. Upward is your bloom.

66

Finding Power In Uncertainty

Certainty is addictive. Tricking ourselves into believing we know something 100% is the ultimate chill pill. It helps us make concrete plans, as if we can predict our uncertain futures. Most people wait for the confidence that comes from being reassured before they actually act. Yet, confidence isn't a requisite of action. Finding power in uncertainty is a superpower.

Creating will take you through changes. It's not a smooth process of sitting in lotus position beneath a Bodhisattva tree as the musings wash over you in a gentle zephyr. Creativity is disruptive. It's very existence is disruptive to the path of what has existed before. The process asks you to try something new, be brave and abandon the tried and true. This goes against our natural instincts; we don't want to try something new and fail. We want to do what we know works and win. To gamble on your gut and take a risk on yourself will, undoubtedly, result in anxiety, frustration and confusion. These feelings can be the exact fuel you need to find power in uncertainty.

First, are you even failing?

Anxiety can be an opportunity to pay closer attention. First, you want to get a handle on whether you're actually failing or if you're just nervous that you are/could be/might be failing. If it's nerves, work through it.

If you're actually failing, you want to fail fast so that you can quickly regroup or completely redirect. The first mistake most people make when they're in crisis is not realizing they're in crisis. The second mistake is panicking when they finally do realize it.

Change is the only constant and nothing was guaranteed to begin with. Don't panic. There are more people in this world guessing their way through life than you realize. Calm down and get over yourself. Failure's going to happen. It's a part of success. You don't learn how to innovate anything by getting everything right all the time.

The opportunity to learn from failure and try again is a privilege of the living and the gifted. Center yourself and start figuring out what you need to learn, unlearn and relearn. Then take action.

Is more creativity required?

Frustration is a call to create and challenge. Nothing happens from sitting on the sofa steeping in your vexation. It's always easier to be a critic than a creator. Dig deeper. Try a new viewpoint and look at the situation from the angle of opposition. Start at the end and think backwards. Mix it up. Don't rest in critique. Criticize by creating. Creativity is a cure for frustration.

Are you focused on the right thing?

Confusion is a chance to seek more/better info and clarity. Asking yourself the right questions and focusing on the right areas is crucial. When our focus is off and we're looking at the wrong strategy, getting busy with the wrong activities and listening to the wrong guidance, we get confused. We can also get confounded when we're not acknowledging our unique skills, acumen and networks that can naturally help us with access and opportunities. Sometimes, the solution requires reaching inward and tapping our natural abilities or reaching out to the network we've already amassed.

If we get too confused, we stand still. Focusing on the things that make sense is one way to move forward. This requires deep digging into what you want, what's working and what isn't, which connections and contacts you've forgotten or are not seeing, and where the narrative is lacking. The rest of the clarity and confidence will come as momentum builds and attracts more momentum.

Often we wait for *certainty* when *synchronicity* is what's really needed.

Synchronicity isn't about *knowing*. It's really about being open to *learning*.

67

Cultivating Synchronicity

Synchronicity: the simultaneous occurrence of events that appear significantly related but have no discernible causal connection. In other words, things start coming together. Grace. Alchemy. Opportunity meeting Preparation. It's that feeling of being in flow, things are going your way and falling into place. You know that problems still exist, but now, somehow, you see solutions everywhere.

This might sound like synchronicity is about knowing, but it's actually about learning. You become more open to possibility, insight and input. It's the secret weapon that arises from embracing the never-ending presence of uncertainty. Even though there's no way to actually know, you trust that your skillset, acumen, social networks, ingenuity and resiliency can figure it out.

Synchronicity doesn't just occur when surprise opportunities fall into our laps. It also happens when we embrace the act of thinking as a collaborative process. We say the right thing to the right person at the right time and suddenly, you find the keys to exactly what you need.

Seek Mentors. Get mentors who are older than you, younger than you and your peers in age. Different stages of life come with their own unique perspectives that are essential for problem solving. I'll even argue that putting them all together can help you better see around corners. Complexity is an advantage and aids synchronicity. Think about it like you're looking at a city. There's streetview and aerial view but there's also all the invisible infrastructure. Complexity offers a fuller picture.

Probe Deeper. When we ask our mentors deeper questions, we have the opportunity for more magical answers.

Discomfort Yourself. Pain points can be great inspiration for critical thinking. Your comfort zone isn't required to feel like you're in flow. It's often about thriving in your element while using discomfort to discover the next move. The pain points are what drive you to search for new answers and ask your trusted inner circle unexpected questions.

Be Open. Keeping an open mind helps you make sense of new information and connections. It might not immediately click, for every moment isn't a eureka-moment, but it will help you consider. Thinking without also dreaming limits your legacy.

Help Others. Sometimes helping someone else problem solve connects the dots on what's troubling you. It stretches you out, and helps you clearly see what was previously hidden. Since your perspective is different from the outside, solutions often seem more abundant and evident.

68

Generational Gifts Further Legacy

Charles Loloma used his unique perspective to change North American jewelry design. I'm rather obsessed. Considered the "Father of New Native American Jewelry", this Hopi artist and designer gained international regard for his modernist approach. Loloma looked like a superstar, with gorgeous hair, cool glasses and a kind of tailored ease about himself. He played with textures, dimensions, colors, mystery, and his Hopi cultural heritage to tell stories through the jewelry he created.

In one ring, Loloma crafted a textured gold band with a small oval opening exposing a bright blue spot of lapis. This minimalistic loveliness is compelling, but the outside expression of this ring is only half of its story. The band's interior reveals a carousel of colored stones only the wearer would know exists as the piece is being worn. It's a secret understanding of what lies beneath and the delight of discovery. It's about digging deeper than the shiny surface and recognizing the universe within. In one simple ring, Loloma uses the brilliance of gold to enhance the allure of natural stones and the allure of life's abundant hidden happenings.

We discover things that have been existing for thousands of years longer than ourselves, name them, and try to make sense of them through our actual senses. That's just who we are. This quote from Loloma gives insight towards a harmonious and creative approach to this process:

> "I felt a strong kinship to stones, not just the precious and semi-precious stones I use in my jewelry, but the humble stones I pick up at random while on a hike through the hills. I feel the stone and think, not to conquer it, but to help it express itself."

This idea of not striving to overpower and overwhelm is revolutionary. His use of mystery is revelatory in the 21st century, for this century's beginnings distrusts the hidden and craves transparency. Social media posts hold back nothing. Exposure is sought for exposure's sake. Everything is being called out and questioned. None of this negates the value of mystery. Humans need play in order to learn.

Loloma died in 1991 at the age of 70. His pieces are widely collected by celebrities, socialites and dignitaries. Bracelets currently sell at auction for upwards of $15,000 U.S. Rings easily go for $20,000 through dealers. The value is in his design aesthetic, his artistry, and — just as individually — his perspective.

Some argue that he's not just the most influential Native American jewelry designer, but also the most influential American one. He drew from an understanding of life that he had gathered through his culture. His collective culture and visionary individualism helped him create something rather commonplace, such a ring, in an extraordinary way. His perspective combined with his talents and skills is what changed everything.

There's buzz about intergenerational curses, but we also have intergenerational gifts. List them out. Know them and appreciate them. Then probe into your vision and see if you've incorporated these gifts into your strategy and work. Don't worry about your personal expression being considered mainstream. Your specificity is already more mainstream than you realize. It just has to be released into the zeitgeist.

69

Self Care Is a Leadership Skill

"Self-care" hit an all-time high as a Google search term after the 2016 US Presidential election. Since then, it's seeing steady growth in countries like Ethiopia, Kenya, Canada, Singapore and Australia. The idea of self-care has been around for decades, first in a medical context and then as a political act by women of color during the civil rights movement. The poet Audre Lorde encouraged radical self care for those battling systems of oppression and illuminated, "Caring for myself is not self-indulgence, it is self-preservation, and that is an act of political warfare."

Now, the idea is trending as a method of giving particular attention to one's well-being. For something that's so necessary to our overall health, it also seems difficult to practice, especially in leadership.

Self care is the most underrated leadership skill. When we talk about caring for ourselves, we're really referring to the gift of self-compassion. This human need to be empathic and compassionate toward yourself goes beyond bubble baths and pampering massages. It embodies a relentless devotion to self-awareness. It requires a deep dedication to creating balance from the inside out as opposed to pursuing perfection from the outside in.

Whenever you are creating, you're leading. You're asserting your experience as an authority on human experience. You're establishing validity and veracity to inspire others to see more and do more. The heart of leadership in developing people, not diminishing them. If you don't prioritize self-compassion, and therein, prioritize self-care, that lack will corrupt your message, your media results and your community building. It will become apparent that you don't embody what you preach; you don't walk your talk. Most importantly, you'll make mistakes simply because you're exhausted. You'll trust the wrong allies and confidants, you'll employ the wrong help, and you won't find the type of duplication you need to free up your time. You'll be unprepared for interviews or lose track of talking points or even get conversationally cornered into sticking your foot in your mouth.

None of this works without self compassion. When we start to acquire and achieve the things we've longed for, struggled towards, and strived for, well, that's when the real work begins. Sustainability isn't about maintaining the status quo or your status in general. It's about growth with as much equilibrium as possible.

The more you can prepare your mindset ahead of time, the less internal strife you experience through the twists and turns of success, expectations, and obligations. You will be kind to yourself more often than not, forgive yourself and grant yourself room to change. You'll also know that your happiness is in healthy relationships with people, not endless dedication to the doing of tasks. This will help you discover balanced resiliency and pass it on to others.

70

In Case You Get Bored

Success leads to growth and, usually, more people becoming dependent upon you remaining successful in a very specific way. This is part of why our world exaggerates the value of specialization. The systems make it precious because it's predictable. Specialization helps us know a lot about a very small slice of experience and that can get some of us very stuck.

There are folks who want to wake up each day and paint. Then there are those of us who want to paint for an entire decade but then, quite suddenly, explore the artistic eye through film directing, or photography, or interior design. Some would rather veer in a dramatically different direction and explore something like anthropology.

If there's talent to do all these different things, but the systems of success to which you've grown accustomed don't welcome such divergence, you might have a problem. You might feel suckered and stagnated. Everything you're doing suddenly feels like a rut and you might want to swerve out of your lane.

People will say you're delusional and stupid. They'll predict such change will fail. They might be right. Others will praise and encourage you. They'll foresee tremendous growth. They might be wrong. Some might even accuse you of being self-destruct and blowing up your life just to break free of the expectations. If that's true, then you've really reached disillusionment with your life and should probably seek therapy instead of destroying everything.

If this is just risk and self-destruction, then no one can decide for you if the risk is worth it. Think of all the times you swore you were losing and you were actually winning. Things weren't falling apart. You just couldn't predict the future. You still can't. So if you're going to make a change, make a plan, devote time to building the lanes for change, and see what happens. Do the work necessary to drastically shift your life such as learning the needed skills, gaining the right mentors and making contacts in new areas of endeavor. Stop assuming you've plateaued.

If your goal doesn't materialize as is, amend it or abandon it. The media system won't care either way. As long as you keep protecting the information you need to protect, and promoting what you can promote through paid, earned, shared, and owned avenues, you'll keep seeing media results.

71

So, You've Become Attached?

If you get caught up in it, you'll get messed up by it. There is no crystal ball. We're all guessing, it's just that some of us are making educated guesses. Our life choices take us down certain paths that then lead to more choices, constantly branching off here and there. When we gain success, it helps us feel certain. For why would things have worked out if it wasn't somehow blessed and sure?

The end-of-history illusion is a phenomena that happens after we experience significant growth but then, for some reason, believe that growth has plateaued. We're never done. What we'll be interested in 10 years from now might not appear before us until 9 years, 364 days from now. One moment can open a new universe in our minds.

Comfort feels great and we all get attached to it. Things start to get routine to build turnkey systems around yourself. Your team relies on this predictability so that they can plan and implement.

Then, one day, you want to swerve out of your lane and do something completely different with your career/public image/messaging. This is bad news for the conservationist among you. It's scary, unknown, disruptive doom that might end all the progress thus far. The problem is, you believe it's time to grow. You believe even if no one else does.

You can't remain where you've outgrown. You also can't swerve on a whim without being irresponsible. Switching lanes requires thought and work. Assuming that you've done the self-work necessary to switch things up, you still need to prepare your media strategy and prepare your team.

Change requires steady monitoring. I always appreciate leaders who cultivate calm during change. The team has a better chance of thinking through everything. That requires deep but clear communication.

You and your community are interdependent. This ecosystem includes you and your message, your team members and inner circle of confidants, companions and collaborators, the larger community you serve, and the ambassadors and stakeholders. Changing times affects all these groups and the less direct control the group members have over said change, the more vulnerable they can feel due to shifts. Clearly and concisely communicating urgency, direction, and trajectory without transferring trauma and chaos will help members accept and navigate the new landscape.

When things are moving fast, we have a tendency to get busy and tired, then we start asking the wrong people to do necessary things. This is so dangerous to a strong, dedicated team. You disrupt things even further when you ask talent to step away from where it thrives. It feel diminishing and disheartening. If things are changing, don't take your talented team members out of their element. You're supposed to be developing them, not dehumanizing them. Whether they work for you or with you, they're aligned with you. Alliances don't work without respect. So delegate properly and hire extra help as needed.

Also, come to community you serve with some details already outlined. You're moving through deep layers of transformation around your work and vision. First, reshape your messaging in a way that it honors the evolution. Make the necessary adjustments to your media plan and goals. Think through everything, because new variations require new plans. Communicate to your team. Figure out what to test in small samplings to the community. Listen for their responses to your new messaging.

With our technology, listening has a wider meaning. We can use online polls and questionnaires in the digital space, monitor

Google analytics and social network analytics on content, and crowdsource opinion through message boards. In real life, we can also create events and panels to provide information and gain insight.

Once you understand how to frame your media for your community, you can approach ambassadors and overall stakeholders with the new packaging. Stay engaged with your inner circle by:

- Updating the team about the climate and situation without bombarding and overloading people's senses.
- Checking in with the team's stress level.
- Taking breaks and providing breaks for the team.
- Be clear with your directives.

Stay engaged with yourself by creating your own mantras from your core beliefs and new goals. Write them out and put them on the wall. Constantly remind yourself of your focus and shift so that you can stay centered while you center others.

Investing in yourself requires belief in your future self. You also have to believe in the future of others and your community's ability to shift over time.

72

Amp Up the Allure

EXERCISE #4
PLAYING WITH LIFE'S LITTLE MYSTERIES

I once threw a party for 400 people without ever *publicizing* the location. To promote a new residential high-rise to a highly-coveted crowd of jet setting trendsetters, I needed a plan that employed mystery and insider access. I created matte black postcards with crisp white typography on both sides. One side stated the date. The other side stated the time. The logo of the building was actually printed on one side of the card in tiny raised black ink against the black background. The entire technique was very statement making with subtle clues. I then told three well-connected people who also had a tendency to quickly spread information my secret, "Don't tell anyone, but I've been so busy throwing this huge party for..." These three key people effectively spread the news about the location for me to that desirable group of potential clientele for the building.

Allure is a powerful thing. Secrets are sexy. They form bonds and feelings of belonging. They make the mundane moments a little more exclusive. Yes, we demand and praise transparency, but we also love how play keeps our minds sharp and blood pumping. Life feels dull without the occasional game.

1. What are the areas of mystery and wonder within your mission or vision?

2. How can you turn these aspects into play and intrigue? Can you create contests or treasure hunts, either figuratively or literally, that invite discovery and discussion around these nuggets?

3. Can you crowdsource ideas and deeper knowledge in ways that invite participation from your community and energizes their oxytocin in the process?

4. Are you open to letting others play with the allure? Can your ego allow it to find its own life?

73

Living Well

All capital is an energy exchange. Capital is the only tool we have to help sustain a legacy. Everything you love requires money and mouths to thrive. It needs social capital and social reach, funding and assets in order to have staying power.

If you have contacts within your network that you hesitate to reach out to for support, then you might not really want what you claim to desire. You can't bring something to life and then refuse to give it the oxygen it needs to survive and thrive. For a legacy, funding is the oxygen.

By the time Francois Marie Arouet de Voltaire was 40, he was independently wealthy. Known throughout history as Voltaire, the philosopher/historian/writer never shut up about social reform, the separation of church and state, and the value of civil liberties. He was walking around making statements like, "It is dangerous to be right in matters of which the established authorities are wrong," and, "If you want to know who controls you, look at who are not allowed to criticize." Since he was living in the 18th century, these thoughts were rather revolutionary.

That's probably how he ended up heavily influencing both the American Revolution and French Revolution.

Being a thinker, Voltaire looked at himself, then looked at his environment, and astutely realized he was a total troublemaker. Any given day of the week, his words might land him in jail or exile. In 1717, he was first exiled and then imprisoned in the Bastille for writings that were offensive to those in power. He was just 23 years old.

His only possible protection for his opinions would be financial sovereignty. Once solvent and self-funded, he could say what he needed and be free of the pesky stress around making enough money to stay alive. He wouldn't have to financially suffer for his art, since plenty of suffering could easily befall him from the ruling class.

Many scholars love to discuss how Voltaire ~~scammed~~ outsmarted the lottery systems of the 1700s, but he also relied on mentors to help him build wealth from those winnings. He developed friendships with affluent bankers such the brothers Paris, four brothers who were all financiers under Louis XIV and Louis XV. These mentors taught him how to invest army supplies and other commodities, speculate in currencies, and grow his money into long-term passive income streams.

Once a millionaire, he was able to become a financier himself. He invested in international trade ships, art and foreign bonds. He even offered direct lending to his customers when they needed purchasing lines of credit.

If he ever had to make a run for it, he had a plan for that too. Voltaire squirreled away money in other nations where it earned interest and dividends in the local currency. This kept him from being dependent upon any single economy and guaranteed he would continue to live well if he ever had to flee political or social persecution.

Voltaire didn't just amass financial capital; he grew his social capital, too. Through financial freedom, Voltaire was able to travel within exclusive social circles. He enjoyed a friendship with inventor Benjamin Franklin, who also had a deep appreciation for the freedom money can bring. He spent 15 years taking residence in a chateau owned by his lover and collaborator, Madame du Châtelet. This residency saved him considerable expense that he would later put into his own property.

By the time he was 55, Voltaire was earning roughly 125,000 francs a year, or what by today's measurements would be close to $938,000 U.S. annually. He continued to speak out against the French judicial system, went on to publish *Candide* and even acquired his own home. So while he was creating content, building media presence, writing letters to roughly 1,500 different people, maintaining press relationships, and declaring, "God gave us the gift of life; it is up to us to give ourselves the gift of living well," Voltaire was enacting a plan for himself. While he spent 40 years being France's dominant playwright, he spent over 20 years investing in lucrative army supplies alone. He created and he invested. For him, money was the tool and freedom was the natural result.

Voltaire was operating before the age of credit scores and accredited investors, but lessons can still be drawn. Looking at your future with an entrepreneurial spirit, humanist heart, and investor mindset helps you leverage all of your work and assets for passive income.

Passive income usually comes from being an investor. Sheer

hourly work for hourly wages and exchanging your physical time for income will rarely result in true financial freedom. Duplication builds capital, and passive income streams are a way to duplicate your wealth. You don't have to wait until you have a vault of money to invest in passive income. You can always start small.

You might need to get a financial advisor or mentor. You might also need to apply different usage to something you already have. I once helped a client build his mailing list to over 10,000 subscribers through networking, online contests and exclusive download offers. As an illustrator, he had tons of content but he also made sure to share poignant industry news in his newsletters, too.

Through an online marketplace, he then started selling e-blasts, or advertised email campaigns, to brands for $125 per campaign. He'd never distribute more than 3 branded e-blasts to his audience per month resulting in an additional $375 in revenue each month. Here's where things shifted.

He then reinvested the ad revenue into building 4 more lists of equal size, which meant $1,875 per month. He put half his winnings into growing more business through commission-based sales reps and invested the other half in himself so that he'd have more time for his art. Meanwhile, the mailing lists he built and segmented helped him keep spreading timely news about his work, grow deeper brand relationships and a more dedicated community that actively shared his content and work. Some of the brands with which he developed a rapport also thousands of dollars into sponsoring real world events for him. That's a lot of growth from such a humble launch pad.

Thinking about passive income requires a luxury mindset of

seeing abundance in your limited resources. It's about making money and knowing how to reinvest it. With a little savvy, vision and patient persistence, your resources beget more resources.

74

Extra Is Beautiful

Years before George Washington became the president of the United States in 1789, he was a younger man running his first campaign in Virginia for the House of Burgesses. He lost by 231 votes. His opposition had lubricated voters with rum, whiskey and beer. Back then, this was perfectly legal and a key part of campaign strategy. It was a voting tradition to binge drink and the candidate with the most liquor flowing would win.

Washington learned his lesson quickly. On the next try, he spent his entire campaign budget of 50 pounds on 116 gallons of booze which he served to 391 voters. He won.

Over 235 years later, a man with the stage name Jay-Z was in a career transition from being a drug dealer to becoming a world famous rapper. He and Roc-a-Fella records entered the music industry with a lot of financial resources, largely due to Jay-Z's primary occupation. Gifting the audience could actually be part of their marketing plan. At the end of stage performances, the music label would throw a thousand dollars of loose money into the excited crowd.

Much like the "voting day" beers in Colonial times, the financial gifting became legend. It helped Jay-Z and Damon Dash be seen as bosses. They gained even more street cred and people crowded the performances. The gifting served as proper word of mouth and laid the foundation of popularity that would later turn into Roc-a-Fella branded merchandise.

Extra is beautiful. Giving a little lagniappe to your audience grows community. Folks get excited. You get reinvigorated. Word of mouth builds more salience and allure amplifies.

The audience you attract from gifting are drawn to the receiving aspect. So, there's a large possibility that they won't be loyal if the generosity ends. This isn't your concern. People kept watching Oprah whether she was giving away cars or not.

Gifting is one aspect of a larger approach. It's a great way to break up the monotony of over-marketing and messaging. Use it but space it out. Have it well-timed. If it makes sense, have it include a clear call to action, such as Washington's "vote for me" beers. When possible, team up with brands and allies to create even bigger giveaways that are exclusive to your community. This can help your budget go further.

Your *ego* **is either** *your tool* **or** *your master.*

Remember *Yourself.*

75

Fortify Your Windows

Someone once stated something along the lines of, "To avoid criticism *say nothing, do nothing,* be nothing." I claim *someone* because no one is really sure who authored it. It's often misattributed to the Greek philosopher Aristotle.

It's possible that the quote is paraphrased from Elbert Hubbard, who — while essaying about an assassination attempt on abolitionist William H. Seward — wrote in 1898, "If you would escape moral and physical assassination, do nothing, say nothing, be nothing." Regardless of the phrase's origins, it rings true. Oblivion is the only perfectly effective pathway to avoid critics, and there's still always the chance that they'll complain about you being so obscure.

If you go about doing things in this life, you're going to attract warranted as well as undeserving criticism. Your words and your actions will misunderstood at some point, and you may not be given ample room to explain yourself. You're going to have moments where you do everything right and it seems the world still wants to kick you in the teeth. You're also going to have moments when you're disturbingly wrong and rightfully getting called to the carpet.

Like change, crisis comes with life. The first mistake most people make when they're in a crisis is, well, not realizing they're in crisis. The second mistake is panicking when they do finally realize it.

So, Rule #1: Don't Panic. Crisis is not the time to start making all your decisions based on fear and the inability to think. The first thing you must do is stay calm and have the audacity to imagine your future self will exist intact.

Even when you're at the center of a crisis, the situation is about much more than you. This is stressful for everyone, especially the people who care about you and depend on you the most. Stay focused.

Ask:

- Can you hire help?
- Can you isolate or stabilize the narrative/issue?
- Can you go silent in the media and public eye until help arrives?
- Can you make sure your team also stays silent during that time?
- Can you establish a core team to handle the situation?
- Can you establish a key contact person or group from that core team to handle information and communication flow?
- Can you avoid doing anything rash?

Throughout this experience, be cognizant of stress and fatigue. The moment will test your metal and resilience. This is why it's never a good idea to handle your own crisis. Consultants and strategists exist for a reason and help during overwhelming moments.

It can be a great idea to invest in prevention and preparation. Getting media trained periodically can help you maintain the skills for sticking to talking points. It helps you avoid dangerous situations, like an unexpected question during a live interview. It helps you better train your team on how to prevent miscommunication or oversharing with a journalist. It even keeps dumb social media posts from getting published. It also prepares you on how to emotionally handle the first 48 hours of a major crisis. Notice that I stated the training should happen periodically. Media training isn't a one-and-done deal. You need refreshers to keep up with interview trends, new media and changes in cultural tastes.

Since we now live in a world where social media gets people fired locally and vilified globally on evening news, crisis is more noticeable. It's lurking closer than before because more people are living more public lives with public thoughts. Plus, we're all highly skilled at misunderstanding each other. Understanding crisis and planning for it can be the key to keeping a cool head.

76

Keep Rising

"We move from data to information to knowledge to wisdom.. And separating one from the other... knowing the limitations and the danger of exercising one without the others, while respecting each category of intelligence, is generally what serious education is about." — TONI MORRISON

By now, we know that not all information is good information. Details and tidbits have quality. There is data, information, knowledge, wisdom, and even collective illumination. Our work involves seeking, finding and deciphering. What we find can disrupt us, wake us, and heal us. We can't only question what we noticeably despise.

We also have to question anything with which we over-identify. Any connection that feels like an exact mirror can become a blindspot. It can keep us from calling upon ourselves. It might exhaust us within the work of building. It may encourage us to not show up for ourselves or mislabel the source of our anxiety. It makes us too eager to find power in a scapegoat or only half-solve a problem.

When we hear the word "mastery," we imagine flawlessness.

This word makes us forget that life is imperfect perfection. Our true mastery is allowing a process of learning, unlearning, and relearning while doing our best to remain calm. We have to remember that at all times we are whole and healing beautifully.

As we heal, we rise into our power. My wish for you is that you always find abundance within yourself and discernment within your support bases. In your most confusing moments, I hope your courage and self compassion serve as your roadmaps. May your inner peace root so deeply that your actions inevitably spring forth from it.

YOU DESERVE TO BECOME MORE THAN A BRAND LIVE YOUR LEGACY

Bibliography

Chilton, Karen. "Hazel Scott's Lifetime of High Notes." Smithsonian.com, 15 Oct 2009. Retrieved from https://www.smithsonianmag.com/arts-culture/hazel-scotts-lifetime-of-high-notes-145939027/

Davidson, Ian. *Voltaire: A Life*. 2nd Edition. 12 Mar 2012. Pegasus Books. USA.

Dunning, Ryanne (Producer). (2018). "*A&E Investigates Cults and Extreme Beliefs*," [Television series], U.S.: A&E Television.

EtrofOnaip. "Hazel Scott in the Army(Hazel in Caisson Number)." Online video clip. YouTube, 22 Feb 2010. Retrieved from https://www.youtube.com/watch?v=EIbGicroCSc

Farokhmanesh, Megan. "Logan Paul controversy highlights the carelessness of online celebrity in the YouTube era." TheVerge, 2 Jan 2018. Retrieved from https://www.theverge.com/2018/1/2/16841260/logan-paul-youtube-suicide-controversy-carelessness-online-celebrity

Freyd, Jennifer J. *Betrayal Trauma: The Logic of Forgetting Childhood Trauma*. 6 February 1998. Harvard University Press. USA.

FORA.tv. "Dunbar's Number: Why We Can't Have More Than 150 Friends." Online video clip. YouTube, 16 Mar 2010. Retrieved from https://youtu.be/ppLFce5uZ3I

Greenstreet, Rosanna. "Yayoi Kusama: 'A letter from Georgia O'Keeffe gave me the courage to leave home'." The Guardian, 21 May 2016. Retrieved from https://www.theguardian.com/lifeandstyle/2016/may/21/yayoi-kusama-interview-artist

History.com Editors. "Mahalia Jackson, the Queen of Gospel, puts her stamp on March on Washington." A&E Television Networks, 13 Nov 2009, Updated 26 Aug 2019. Retrieved from https://www.history.com/this-day-in-history/mahalia-jackson-the-queen-of-gospel-puts-her-stamp-on-the-march-on-washington

Lenz, Heather (Director, Screenplay). (13 Sep 2018). *KUSAMA: INFINITY*. Magnolia Pictures, USA.

Mack, Dwayne. "Hazel Scott: A Career Curtailed." The Journal of African American History, Vol. 91:, Issue 2,: pages 153-170.

NCC Staff. "Booze on Election Day was an American tradition." National Constitution Center, 2 Nov 2012. Retrieved from https://constitutioncenter.org/blog/booze-on-election-day-was-an-american-tradition/

Pandey, Erica. "Sean Parker: Facebook was designed to exploit human "vulnerability"." Online video clip. Axios, 9 November 2017. Retrieved from https://www.axios.com/sean-parker-facebook-was-designed-to-exploit-human-vulnerability-1513306782-6d18fa32-5438-4e60-af71-13d126b58e41.html

Paul, Logan (@LoganPaul). "Dear Internet," 7:00PM, 1 Jan 2018. Tweet. Retrieved from https://twitter.com/LoganPaul/status/948026294066864128/photo/1

Pearson, Roger. "Voltaire's Luck: The French philosopher outsmarts the lottery." Lapham's Quarterly. Retrieved from https://laphamsquarterly.org/luck/voltaires-luck/

Pearson, Roger. *Voltaire Almighty: A Life in the Pursuit of Freedom.* 7 Nov 2005. Bloomsbury USA. USA.

Scheftel, Jeff (Director). (1997). *MAHALIA JACKSON - THE POWER AND THE GLORY: THE LIFE AND MUSIC OF THE WORLD'S GREATEST GOSPEL SINGER.* [Motion Picture], USA.

Scutts, Joanna. "This Piano Prodigy Was the First African-American Woman to Host Her Own TV Show." Time.com, 27 Sept 2016. Retrieved from https://time.com/4507850/hazel-scott/

BIBLIOGRAPHY

Trendacosta, Katharine. "How Fan Art Brought Olivia Munn's Psylocke to *X-Men: Apocalypse*." Gizmodo, 11 May 2016, 4:15PM. Retrieved from https://i09.gizmodo.com/how-fan-art-brought-olivia-munns-psylocke-to-x-men-apo-1776098911

Vincent, James. "YouTuber Logan Paul apologizes for filming suicide victim, says 'I didn't do it for views'." TheVerge, 2 Jan 2018, Retrieved from https://www.theverge.com/2018/1/2/16840176/logan-paul-suicide-video-apology-aokigahara-forest

Valdesolo, Piercarlo & DeSteno, Dave. (2011) Synchrony and the Social Tuning of Compassion

Vieceli, Julian & Shaw, Robin N. (2010) Brand salience for fast-moving consumer goods: An empirically based model, Journal of Marketing Management, 26:13-14, 1218-1238, DOI: 10.1080/0267257X.2010.523009

Vieceli, Julian & Shaw, Robin. (2011). A model of brand salience.

Vieceli, Julian & Shaw, Robin. "An Analysis of the Involvement—Commitment Relationship across Product Categories." Retrieved from https://pdfs.semanticscholar.org/a390/ba52571c2916cc4c8bcb05e1f3e46e63ba98.pdf

BIBLIOGRAPHY

Waddell Gallery. "Charles Loloma." Sub-reference: "American Master of Stone." Retrieved from https://waddellgallery.com/collections/charles-loloma

The Wall Street Journal. "How Martin Luther King Went Off Script in 'I Have a Dream'." Online Video Clip. YouTube, 24 Aug 2013. Retrieved from https://youtu.be/KxlOlynG6FY

Acknowledgments

A decade before I began writing this book, I was shaping it with my work, public speaking, and life experiences. The entire time, I've bombarded the minds and peace of my inner circle with my observations, questions, confusions, and curations. I'd like to thank my husband, Jeff Moeller, for always encouraging my light and supporting this long journey. You lent ears and eyes, perspective and commentary that helped me think and create. Zalika Sapp-Weaver, thank you for being my sister, forever having my back, and helping me see around corners, beneath bedrock, and across solar systems. Rodney Charles and African Artists Association, my deepest gratitude to you for inviting me to speak at AFI. Our Q&A encouraged me to write this book. Julian Ufano-Leon, thanks for our breakfast and coffee chats about neuro-linguistic reprogramming, subconscious thought, and how we place our subconscious in our companion technologies. Dr. Nicole Haggard, thank you for your energy and acumen. Your research on the intersections of race, sex and Hollywood gave me deeper insight into the stories we've told and sold. Munika Lay, thank you for your creativity and brilliant organizational mind. My time with you has reinforced how valuable it is to have collaborative thought. A big thanks to Tabby Biddle and Elisa Henderson Parker; the cohort experience that you two co-directed has helped me remember the rare and wondrous feeling of *true support*. Kristen Isaac, thank you for understanding my vision and helping me design my media map. Kristen Nedopak, you are a warrior queen and your dedication to the creative process inspires me everyday. Will Armstrong, thank you for always spreading my name around town and being so full of life. Kathy Eldon, you brought the term "creative activist" into my life and it broadened my vocabulary for my own life. For that, I'm eternally grateful. Kim Kenny, thank you for providing me platform and inspiration. Kimberlyn Carter, thank you for sending out waves of support that keep me light and lifted. Finally, thank you to my folks, James and Lola Donnell and Lionel Blakeney for helping me realize life is more fun when you don't put a roof on yourself.

Also By Joy Donnell

Pitch Perfect

Own Your Power

Notebook

Notebook

Notebook

Notebook

Notebook

Notebook

Notebook

A Conversation With Joy Donnell

Q: *Beyond Brand* is your second book. Discuss how this project compares with *Pitch Perfect*. Was one more challenging or difficult to write than the other? Did you have to be more vulnerable in certain areas?

A: *Beyond Brand* and *Pitch Perfect* both drew from my work history and personal experiences of helping others build prominence in the media. The books are 10 years apart and *Beyond Brand* is particularly informed by my inner devotion to well-being while navigating this more media-driven, polarized landscape. The ways my projects and perspective have expanded are a direct result of the various ways society has started asking different questions of ourselves and our media.

I wrote *Pitch Perfect* when social media was slowly getting everyone's attention. I remember pitching big studios about ways their platform strategies needed to ramp up and, at the time, they didn't feel a sense of urgency. Now, it's all everyone talks about and thinks about. Personal branding is a much larger buzzword. Celebrity has taken on new levels of meaning. All these cultural shifts and possibilities are deeply discussed in *Beyond Brand* and ultimately, the book looks to have a 360° conversation about public image, leadership, and a full human experience.

Q: Why do you feel legacy, as opposed to branding, is the new/ now/ next conversation of the 21st century?

A: Our human history shows that many people have been denied a sense of legacy within their families, communities and countries due to prejudice, bigotry, racism, sexism and other forms of societal neglect. Our institutions are no longer trusted. People naturally want to reclaim their self-determination and that requires legacy, not just branding. People are thinking about how their actions today can benefit future generations. Again, that's legacy. Creative disruptors are using their gifts with the sole purpose of giving voice to the voiceless, highlighting what has been buried or ignored, and building longer tables in key decision-making rooms. That's a sense of legacy.

Q: Tell us about what drove you to work in media.

A: I've always been a storyteller. That instinct first led me to PR and branding where I was shaping the narrative for entertainment and luxury campaigns. I was always creating media for clients and crafting it with a full content strategy, only, I never thought of the work in that way. I just called it PR. Looking back, it's funny that I didn't see what I was doing since I had pursued this type of storytelling because of a personal failure.

While in college, I was leading a social action campaign f or a Somali women seeking refuge for herself and her daughter. Her daughter didn't want to be circumcised, which is a common practice in certain parts of Somalia. Her mother got her out of the country and when I heard the story, I thought the solution would be so easy... I literally started a petition. Of course, that didn't work at all. That's not even close to how the world works. In that moment, I realized that I didn't understand anything about anything. I needed to gain a better knowledge of storytelling and the human-made, as well as, neurological systems through which our stories resonate. That goal became my quest.

Q: How has your work background informed your growth?

A: After several years of doing countless campaigns, luckily, I was restless. I didn't want to solely have the conversations that my clients paid me to have. I wanted to create platforms for deeper discussions. I wanted to tap into the power of media and use it to connect, expand our understanding of ourselves in this world, and increase our humanity. I especially like digital media because you never run out of space. It can be infinite. Which means you can build a longer table, a table as long as it needs to be. I built a luxury digital media outlet, devised and implemented social awareness campaigns, and was able to tell stories I never would have told in my previous career.

Q: On page 150, you mention that "messiness is contagious" and you later discuss the process of preparing your team for change. What connects these concepts and why are they important?

A: Change is the only constant. It's inevitable. Yet, when success happens, people get comfortable and rely on the certainty that comes with knowing what to expect. So change, although natural, can be very stressful. If you're messy with your team, they can easily get off track. There's a difference between being transparent and unloading your mess and internal process on others.

Q: What can we do to make these transitions less

traumatizing?

A: Update the team on the current climate and situation without bombarding and overloading people's senses. Check in with the team's stress level. Take your breaks. Provide breaks for the team. Be clear with your directives. You want to guide the team to new horizons through change because even the smoothest transitions are stressful. That happens by providing them information and bringing them into the process so they can hold space, but protect their energy as best you can. This mutual respect is going to influence how you interact with the media and maintain those relationships during shifts, too.

Q: The word "support" constantly appears and is highly focused on throughout this book. Why do you touch on it so intensely?

A: Whenever you create, you're in a leadership position strictly based on the fact that you're taking initiative to bring something forth into the world. Leadership doesn't make you superhuman. You must create support for yourself so you can support your team. Don't be afraid to get coaches, mentors and take classes since this aids growth. These elements help you stay calm and not panic too much.

Q: How did self awareness and self compassion become part of your life and work?

A: I was so burnt out, I needed a new phrase for burnt out. It was stealing my joy. As I assessed all the things that were going sideways, I realized every mistake and misstep I'd made happened because I was exhausted. So, I started prioritizing self-care. I needed to be centered and fortified, not off-kilter and broken down.

Q: What did you discover?

A: I started to get more work done and produce higher quality results. Self-care keeps my creativity fueled so my ideas, work and happiness actually flow. It also helps me stay appreciative of my accomplishments rather than steeped in my frustrations, which helps me keep falling in love with my work over and over again.

Q: You examine alliances and the idea of delegating. How do these elements factor into owning your power, joy and media?

A: Alliances don't work without respect and when you prioritize them, you delegate in more proper, mindful ways. I've witnessed teams crumble because leadership kept asking people to step away from the areas where they thrive. Why ask your graphic designer to do your accounting? That diminishes talent when you should want to develop it. It works better when you let talent own its space. Don't take it out of its element. Instead, hire extra help when it's needed. The quickest way this factors into media is when I see people ask the wrong team members to pitch them to outlets. It often goes sideways and hurts the fragile process of building trust with media professionals.

Q: How did you become open-minded to opposing viewpoints?

A: One day, I realized that even detractors are providing

feedback and all feedback has useful data. Being open to it gives you a competitive edge since few people tap it as a resource.

Be Social

1. PICK YOUR FAVORITE CHAPTERS AND MEMES
2. SHARE THEM ON SOCIAL MEDIA
3. TAG & USE HASHTAGS

#beyondbrand #heysuperjoy

@doitinpublic

Let us know your thoughts and ideas.

☞ *Connect with Joy Donnell online:*

doitinpublic.com

Twitter: @doitinpublic

Instagram: @doitinpublic

Find SUPERJOY Media:

heysuperjoy.com

Twitter: @heysuperjoy

Instagram: @heysuperjoy

About Beyond Brand

You're human. You deserve to be more than a brand. For those seeking something different, Beyond Brand expands the ideas of your power, inner joy and media outreach to build legacy — a cultural legacy you can live in real-time as well as leave behind.

Through stories, self examination, best practices and strategy, Donnell breaks down how to keep what you create aligned with who you are becoming. She discusses the intrigues of building support systems that help you thrive, messaging that helps you resonate, media planning that leaves room for flexibility, and content that offers you financially viable routes for continued growth.

Humans are creators, change agents, disruptors, and innovators. We're the forces that shift behaviors, environments, and norms. To confine our gifts to finite public images is a disservice to human advancement, a constriction of personal growth, and a small, limiting lifestyle. We can look beyond brand and live our legacy.

About Joy Donnell

Joy Donnell is a producer, brand strategist, author and speaker dedicated to creating media that expands human understanding. She believes in owning your power and for Donnell, power is owning your voice, image, narrative, influence and intentions. Joy's work actively combines publicity, content strategy and media to build legacy and increase awareness.

Her storytelling expertise touches all of her work as she brings that insight to content strategy and content creation. When she isn't behind the camera creating editorials and fashion films as a producer, she steps in front of the camera as a spokesperson. Donnell is Chief Visionary of SUPERJOY Media and currently lives in California. She can be found online at doitinpublic.com

www.ingramcontent.com/pod-product-compliance
Lightning Source LLC
Chambersburg PA
CBHW031428160426
43195CB00010BB/651